George C. Connor

Historical Guide to Chattanooga and Lookout Mountain

with descriptions of the battles, battle-fields, climate, industries, minerals,

timber, etc

George C. Connor

Historical Guide to Chattanooga and Lookout Mountain
with descriptions of the battles, battle-fields, climate, industries, minerals, timber, etc

ISBN/EAN: 9783337287511

Printed in Europe, USA, Canada, Australia, Japan

Cover: Foto ©Andreas Hilbeck / pixelio.de

More available books at **www.hansebooks.com**

HISTORICAL GUIDE

TO

CHATTANOOGA

AND

LOOKOUT MOUNTAIN,

WITH

DESCRIPTIONS OF THE BATTLES, BATTLE-FIELDS, CLIMATE,
INDUSTRIES, MINERALS, TIMBER, ETC.

PROFUSELY ILLUSTRATED.

BY

GEORGE C. CONNOR,

FOR NEARLY TWENTY YEARS A RESIDENT
OF THE CITY.

1889

TO THE STRANGER.

In the preparation of this Guide to Chattanooga and its Environs, the author has been animated by one desire above all others—To tell the truth! This he has tried to do to the best of his ability, avoiding the language of exaggeration, so common in publications of this class.

Strangers visiting this city may rely upon the information given herein. We have gathered it with great care, and have winnowed the facts. It has been a labor of love, and conscientious earnestness. Sincerely desiring a solid, conservative and permanent growth for the city that contains our home, we have carefully rejected all statements that tended to mislead the enquirer.

This GUIDE is a private venture of the author. It contains no advertisements, no puffs, no unmerited commendations. We have written without embarrassment, being under obligations to no one. At first we offered to insert certain cuts free of charge, but as soon as the owners began to feel that they were doing us favors we abandoned the intention. We are, therefore, indebted for patronage or favors to no one.

This much is due the stranger and the author. The Guide is now submitted to the consideration of those who may desire to know and understand Chattanooga.

(5)

CHATTANOOGA.

On the southern bank of the Tennessee River, in Hamilton County, Tennessee, at the mouth of a valley formed by Missionary Ridge on the east and Lookout Mountain on the west, nestles the city of Chattanooga, famous as "Ross' Landing" when the Cherokees inhabited the surrounding mountains, and with its present name in the annals of the late War Between the States.

The city lies in a basin, with mountain walls so securely protecting it that its fruit seasons are equal to those of West Point, Georgia, a point fully 150 miles farther south; fully four weeks in advance of Cincinnati, and nearly two weeks in advance of Nashville and Knoxville.

Rising 1,700 feet above the beautiful Tennessee River, that for miles laves the streets of the city, world-famed Lookout Mountain lifts its hoary head, its "point" of sheer and solid rock, standing out like a mighty sentinel to guard against the approach of evil influences to the pretty valleys on either side. Beyond the river are Raccoon Mountain and Walden's Ridge, and through the chasm which separates these the Tennessee flows out reluctantly from the valley in which it has lingered to plunge through the mountains that separate us from Sequachee. On this side the river is the abrupt elevation known as Cameron Hill, bedecked with cottages, and around its base spreads out the giant city, with broad avenues that are reasonably well shaded, with its tall spires on houses dedicated to the worship of God, its busy and crowded thoroughfares, its outreaching arms of steel on which trains are darting hither and thither, its numerous factories whose smoke hangs over them like a veil, and its pretty houses perched upon the eminences that range around the business quarter.

Chattanooga is peculiarly located. It stands at the apex of an inverted triangle, whose diverging lines extend into the far northeast and northwest. The mountain walls ward off the colder blasts of winter, while they form a funnel through which sweep, from the opposite direction, the cooling breezes of summer. These mountains surrender their bosoms to early fruit raising—peaches, grapes and strawberries, and to early vegetables of every name. There is no city of the Union more attractively surrounded by scenery, or one more liberally provided with habitable mountain tops.

And now, with these few words by way of generalization, let us examine this remarkably prosperous city in detail. And first,

HISTORICAL.

The country extending from the Little Tennessee and Clinch Rivers, on the north, to the Muscle Shoals on the south, and to the Chattahoochee River on the east, was once inhabited by that most warlike tribe of the southern Indians,

(7)

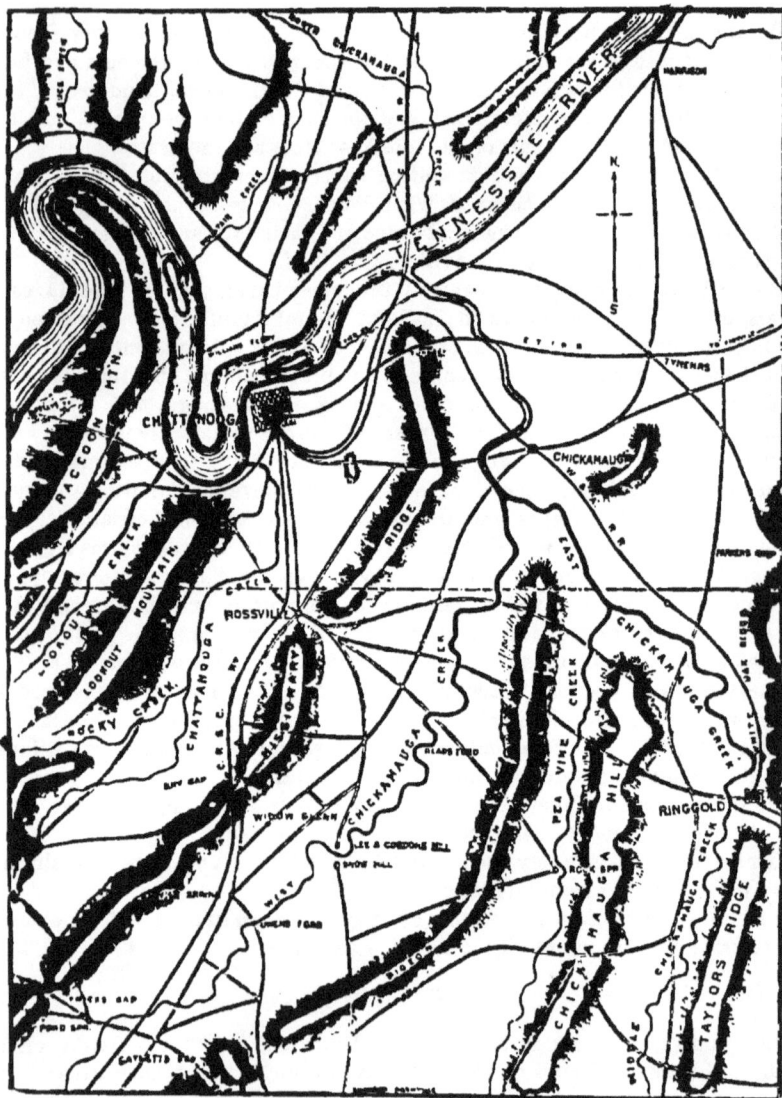

CHATTANOOGA AND THE BATTLE FIELDS.

the Cherokees. Soon after the settlement of the State of Tennessee this tribe was subdued by the white man, and peaceful relations were ever after maintained.

About the year 1817, the American Board of Commissioners for Foreign Missions established a missionary school for the education of the rising generation of the Cherokees, six miles east of Chattanooga, on the Chickamauga. They called it Brainard, in memory of the Rev. David Brainard, an honored missionary to Indians in former years. In 1819 a treaty was made with the Cherokees, whereby they ceded all that territory lying between the Hiawassee and Little Tennessee Rivers, and all of their lands lying north of the Tennessee River, including that part of Hamilton County lying north of that river.

In the latter part of 1835, another treaty was made with these Cherokees, whereby they ceded to the United States all the country they owned east of the Mississippi River, including portions of Georgia, Alabama and Tennessee, for a tract of country west of the State of Arkansas and a bonus of five millions of dollars. This was called the treaty of New Echota, and was made by the Rev. Mr. Schemerhorn, on the part of the United States, and the people of the Cherokee Nation, as it was alleged, on the other part. The great majority of the nation, headed by their chief, John Ross, refused to agree to the treaty, and made strenuous efforts to have it abrogated or modified; but the powers were against them, and they had to yield. In the fall of 1838 the last of the race bade farewell to their native hills and set their faces toward the setting sun.

The site of the present city of Chattanooga was formerly known as Ross' Landing, and after the removal of the Indians it soon assumed the proportions of a trading town, being the entrepot for the products of East Tennessee, and the point from which supplies were drawn for the new settlements of North Georgia and Eastern Alabama. In 1836 it was made a military post, four companies of Tennessee Volunteers, in the service of the United States, being stationed here. These were soon afterward relieved by a portion of the regular army.

The settlement began in 1835, when there was only a forest, and a primitive ferry maintained by the Indian Chief, John Ross, and in a log hut a tavern, kept by mine host, Mr. Daniel Henderson. In 1837 a post-office was established, with John P. Long as postmaster, and the mail came from Rossville on horseback. Later in the year the establishing of the stage line between Murfreesboro, Tenn., and Augusta, Ga., gave the "Landing" office more importance, and letters were actually received from Washington, D. C., within ten days after date.

The struggles of those early times were with natural surroundings and white depravity, the Indians giving the settlers scarcely any trouble whatever. The Cherokees were brave and true to their treaties, and perhaps less treacherous than any of the aboriginal tribes. The few citizens who remain and have memories of those early days tell us quaint stories, which lack of space only forbids us to relate. It may be interesting to record, however, that necessity was never more certainly the "mother of invention" than when W. L. Dugger, as a lad, dragged the timber from Market street to the brick kiln, on Mulberry, with a yoke of oxen, hitched to grape-vines instead of to chains.

In 1838, the town was laid out, when the name Chattanooga was selected, after a lively contest, which occurred in the log school-house that stood on the corner of Fifth and Lookout streets. Lookout City and Montevideo were the names supported by a minority of the citizens. The meaning of "Chattanooga" is unknown. The Cherokees have a tradition that it is the name another race gave to the valley, and also to what we call Lookout Mountain, before they came, and that the Cherokees adopted it without enquiry as to its meaning.

The boundaries of the town, as fixed in 1838, were as follows: On the east by Georgia avenue, and on the west by Cameron hill; on the north by the Tennessee River, and on the south by what was then James street, but now known as West Ninth. The land thus enclosed measured 240 acres.

In 1840, Market street was surveyed, and Tom Crutchfield, Sr., received the timber standing thereon as compensation for opening it. With the timber thus cut he burned the first kiln of bricks on Mulberry street, now known as Broad, and began the erection of two brick residences, one for James A. Whiteside and the other for Dr. Milo Smith.

The year 1840 was one of melancholy memories to those sturdy pioneers. The Tennessee River rose to a great height in the month of June, and when the corn was in tassel overflowed the lowlands, and destroyed the crops. This destruction of vegetation poisoned the air with malaria when the waters receded. A malarial fever immediately broke out, and it soon became epidemic. Before long there were not enough healthy people to wait upon the sick.

Of those early days there remain (1889) only William Crutchfield and George W. Snodgrass, whose cabin on the battle-field of Chickamauga—or Chick-um-au-ga, as the Indians pronounced it—has been made famous.

In 1843 the Legislature took a vote on selecting Chattanooga as the State capital. It was carried in the House, but was lost in the Senate by a majority of two. The capital was then fixed at Nashville. In 1852 the first City Council was chosen, and Dr. Milo Smith was elected Mayor.

It may be important to remember that as early as 1828 a steamboat, called the "Atlas," was run between Muscle Shoals and Knoxville, and that in 1831 the "Knoxville" ran between the same points, and went even higher into East Tennessee than the city of Knoxville.

Quite early in the settlement of Chattanooga there was regular communication by river with New Orleans, except a portage of forty miles around Muscle Shoals, on which a railroad had been built and operated by horse power, between Tuscumbia and Decatur. By this means Chattanooga was enabled to supply the northern counties of Georgia and Alabama with groceries cheaper than from any other point, which, with her East Tennessee productions, gave her a commanding and growing trade.

The first effort at iron manufacture was made about the year 1850. Mr. Hollister, a practical iron master, visited the place, made an examination of the ores and the coal, and was pleased with the prospect. He raised a company and the necessary capital, went North and perfected plans and specifications, but on his way back took sick and died at Charleston. This ended the enterprise. Shortly after this the foundry and car works of the East Tennessee Iron

Manufacturing Company was established, which was afterward bought out by Thomas Webster. The same company erected a blast furnace on the river bank near the bluff, which was afterward leased by James Henderson, of New Jersey, but owing to the want of skill and capital proved a failure. The steam foundry of John G. Bynum was a success, as was also the pork-packing establishments of Chandler & Co. and Joseph Ramsey. The flouring mill of O. E. Granville, with a capacity of fifty barrels a day, and the flouring mill and distillery of Bell & Co., with a capacity of 150 barrels of flour and 60 barrels of whisky a day, were successful until destroyed by the war.

DURING THE WAR.

When the unfortunate civil war began Chattanooga was little more than a straggling village, although it had been dignified by a Mayor and Board of Aldermen during the nine years preceding. Its citizens were divided on the secession of the State, and such bitterness as usually attends religious and political discussions resulted. Houses were divided against themselves.

After Shiloh Chattanooga received the sick and wounded of the Confederates, and after the Fort Donelson defeat the importance of the place from a strategic standpoint was recognized by the Confederate Government. Henceforward it was a depot for supplies. It was attached and again detached as different generals came into command of departments. But it did not assume its greatest importance until Bragg's army came from Tupelo, Miss., and began preparations for the movement into Middle Tennessee and Kentucky in 1862.

Hospitals were scattered here and there, and prisoners were guarded until exchanged or sent to other prisons farther south. The campaign of General Kirby Smith into Kentucky withdrew attention from Chattanooga until Bragg's retreat after Perryville. When Bragg returned to Middle Tennessee Chattanooga was his base of supplies, and the army and floating population became treble the number it was at the opening of the war.

During that time the brilliant but erratic Henry A. Waterson, now the editor of the Louisville Courier-Journal, edited in this city the "Chattanooga Rebel," a daily paper without a counterpart in English literature; a thorn in the flesh to General Bragg, a tonic and delight to the rank and file of his army.

In the last weeks of June, 1863, Rosecrans made a vigorous movement on the Confederate right flank which compelled Bragg to fall rapidly back from Shelbyville upon Chattanooga, the natural gateway from Tennessee to the Atlantic coast. Rosecrans halted at McMinnville and Winchester, and awaited Burnside's march upon Knoxville. Bragg reached Chattanooga on July 7th, and Rosecrans reached Bridgeport, the railroad crossing of the Tennessee, on August 29th. Those outside of the councils of the army innocently supposed Chattanooga could not be captured by the Federals.

TWO IMPORTANT EVENTS.

One of the most successful steps toward the obliteration of the animosities, and the healing of the wounds of the late war, was taken by the Ladies' Confederate Memorial Association when they invited the Federal garrison of this post to unite with the veterans of the Confederacy in laying the corner-stone of the Monument to the Confederate Dead.

It was a charming sunny day, that 10th of May, 1877, when the long procession of Freemasons, Knights Templar, ex-Confederates, citizens and the Ladies' Memorial Association moved down Market and up Sixth streets, en route to the Confederate Cemetery, led by the band of Col. Wheaton's regiment, U. S. Army, and Company C of the same, commanded by Capt. Cochran. And when that United States military band entered the densely shaded City of the Dead, followed by a company of U. S. troops, with arms reversed, there was not a dry eye nor a disloyal heart in the vast throng assembled around the base of the monument, or in the long procession that moved up the avenue. And such a procession at such a time was possible in Chattanooga only.

The next important event was of a like character. The Society of the Army of the Cumberland decided to hold its annual reunion in the city of Chattanooga during Chickamauga week, September 21 and 22, 1881. The writer of this pamphlet conceived the idea of organizing a society of ex-Confederate soldiers to extend a soldierly greeting to the Society of the Army of the Cumberland on the occasion of its visit to us. His most sanguine expectations were realized, a large society was organized, and ex-Confederates of every grade, from general to private, wrote letters of approval and concurrence. The society chose J. B. Cooke to be president, D. M. Key and J. A. Caldwell to be vice presidents. G. C. Connor to be secretary, and W. W. Jackson to be treasurer. S. A. Key was unanimously chosen to deliver the address of welcome, and by joint action of the local committee and this society, Cameron Hill was selected as the most appropriate spot for the ceremonies.

All arrangements were completed when the flash of the telegraph announced *"President Garfield is dead."* It was nearly midnight of September 19th when the tolling bells announced the awful calamity. The programme was in the hands of the printer; the buildings were rapidly assuming their gay decorations; visitors were beginning to arrive; all was bustle and expectation. In an instant a cloud of gloom settled upon every heart. Crape was silently and tearfully pinned to the national colors. The publication of the joyous programme was suspended, and a call issued for a joint conference at ten o'clock the following day.

Next morning the assembly hall was filled with ex-Confederates and Federals, bowed with grief, and solicitous of doing nothing inappropriate to the solemn surroundings. The Society of the Army of the Cumberland decided to hold only the briefest sessions, and the ex-Confederates proposed that the programme adopted for Thursday be carried out on Cameron Hill, the banners and badges draped in mourning, and the ceremonies of the greeting and flag-raising to be succeeded by requiem services. This was unanimously adopted. The Confederates next proposed to surrender their reunion, appointed for Thursday afternoon, and invited the Army of the Cumberland to unite with them at that hour in a Union Memorial Service. This invitation was cordially accepted.

The sun rose into a cloudless sky on Thursday, September 22, 1881. All trains entering the city were packed with visitors. Hundreds came by all kinds of conveyances on the public roads, and by 10 o'clock there were not less than ten thousand strangers in the city. The headquarters of both armies were crowded, and the Reception Committees found it no small matter to keep up the registers.

Promptly at 11 o'clock the two columns were formed at the points announced. At 11.30 these columns united into a grand procession, led by the band of the Fifth Artillery, U. S. A.

The sad death of our beloved President reduced the number of representatives more than one-half. Thousands were *en route* to our city, in hopes of having a jollification of the most patriotic and exhilarating kind, but turned back when they heard of the pall that settled down on Elberon. It did not occur to them that this very sadness would add to the effects of the extraordinary exercises devised for them in Chattanooga. They thought only of mirth and rejoicing at such a gathering, while the people of Chattanooga, with tearful eyes, were draping their homes with mourning, and exchanging the entertaiments and amusements for a requiem and a funeral.

The ceremonies on Cameron Hill we describe in the "Tour of the City," but at 4 o'clock in the afternoon memorial services were held in the court-house square by apppointment of the societies of both armies. An immense throng again assembled and listened to addresses by Gen. Wheeler and Rev. J. W. Bachman, from the Confederates, and Gen Cox, of Ohio, and Gen. Willard Warner, from the Federals. Hon. D. M. Key presided.

This union meeting appointed the following committee, after adopting suitable resolutions, to attend the obsequies of the President, in Cleveland, on the following Monday, viz.: Maj. A. H. Pettibone, Maj. G. C. Connor, Capt. J. M. Thornburg, Capt. M. H. Clift, Capt. H. S. Chamberlain, Rev. Col. J. W. Bachman and E. A. James. The committee met and elected A. H. Pettibone, who was a classmate of the President, chairman, and G. C. Connor, secretary.

On the evening previous to these ceremonies Judge R. H. Cochran, of Wheeling, W. Va., delivered the official oration before the Society of the Army of the Cumberland. So truly did it present the feelings of the ex-Confederates that they unanimously requested it for publication.

☞ At this writing (May, 1889) preparations are again being made for another reunion of the Society of the Army of the Cumberland, in Chattanooga, September next. Our people will welcome those brave men as heartily now as they did in 1881.

POINTS OF WAR INTEREST.

The march of progress, we are happy to say, has blotted out nearly all of the landmarks of the occupations during the civil war. The mighty earthworks have nearly all been leveled, and Forts Wood and Negley have given place to residences. The trenches have disappeared by the processes of erosion, and only in memory do the forts, lunettes, redoubts and batteries announced in General Order No. 63, April 27, 1864, exist.

On the eminence east of the town palatial residences are blotting out every trace of Fort Wood. The huge earthwork that stood on the rising ground west

of the Rossville road, near Montgomery avenue and the Stanton House, has left
a few traces, but they will soon disappear.   Cameron Hill has had the wrinkles
of forts and redoubts smoothed out of its summit and bosom, and the "old reservoir," so often quoted, has turned to dust.

Department headquarters, established by Gen. Rosecrans, and continued by
Gen. Thomas, is now known as 316 Walnut street, and it was there Thomas
welcomed Grant on October 23, 1863.   There the battle of Missionary Ridge was
planned by Grant, Thomas and Sherman.   At 302 Walnut street was the office
of the adjutant general, and at 326 Walnut was the headquarters of the chief of
artillery, Gen. Brannan.   Around the corner, on First street from Walnut, at
No. 110, was Sherman's headquarters.   At 19 East Fourth was the office of the
provost marshal general of the Army of the Cumberland.

These buildings have been but slightly changed since the days of their military occupancy.   We quote them here for the information of the members of the
Army of the Cumberland who are continually visiting the city.

The removal of the heavy forest growth from Cameron Hill and from various
parts of the city changes the aspect from what was seen by the Confederates
when they evacuated, and by the Army of the Cumberland immediately after
the disaster of Chickamauga, and only certain buildings remain as landmarks of
forts and hospitals.   Ex-Confederates will remember the residence as the headquarters of Gen. Bragg, and the large building and fine grounds on the corner
of Pine and Sixth as the headquarters of Gen. D. H. Hill.   This was Gen. Mc-
Pherson's headquarters in Federal days.

The marking of places by the erection of tablets is not to be commended,
since they would be memorials of a fractricidal strife that should be forgotten as
soon as possible.   The descendants of the gallant men on both sides should not
be perpetually reminded that their fathers once were enemies.

AN HISTORIC HOUSE.

On the corner of Market and Fourth streets stands a three-story brick building, the first erected in Chattanooga, and perhaps the only landmark of those
early days with a pathetic history.   Indeed, its seamed, bolted and battered appearance suggests an enquiry to every visitor.

This building was erected in 1840, and is now used by the city for its Council
chamber, its city offices, and police headquarters.   It has been so used since
1883, the year it was purchased by the city.   For six years previously it was
used by the county for like purposes.

Prior to the war the ground floor was used as stores, the second floor as sleeping apartments, and the third as a Masonic hall.   When the Confederates occupied the city they converted the upper floors into a prison, and the lower one
was occupied as military offices, especially by the provost marshal.   There were
oaken floors laid above, to add security to the prison, and into these floors were
driven staples and rings, to which chains were attached, and to the chains the
shackles of the unfortunate prisoners were fastened.   The prisoners, thus
chained, were of all classes; spies, deserters, traitors to the Southern cause, and
criminals.   Even after making allowances for exaggeration, the stories told of

those gloomy rooms are most harrowing. Out of them went gallant fellows to be shot as spies and as "traitors," and criminals to suffer the just decrees of broken laws. The records are lost, and we are glad that they are.

When the Confederates evacuated and the Federals came into possession the tables were turned sure enough, and guards and informers became prisoners, to be watched and punished by those who stood in terror of incarceration only a few weeks before. Spies, deserters and criminals still lay chained to the floor, and brave as well as bad men went to their death as before.

Early in 1864 the block of buildings adjoining the house on the south caught fire, and was destroyed. During the fire a Confederate, charged with being a spy, succeeded in getting out upon the roof, and by superhuman efforts saved his prison. He was released next day for his gallantry.

The close of the war returned this building to its owners in a dilapidated condition, and it was variously used until October, 1877, when it was purchased by the county for court-house purposes, at a cost of $10,000. Something over $7,000 worth of repairs were made. When the court-house was finished this building was vacated, and the city bought it in January, 1883, paying only $6,000. Changes and repairs were made which have brought it to its present appearance; unsightly architecturally, but a landmark worthy of preservation.

A GREAT PROSPERITY.

After the disorders that followed the close of the war had ended, and honest government had assumed control, Chattanooga began to struggle into the light. A mighty effort was made by those interested in the Alabama & Chattanooga Railway to practically remove the business of the city south of the Western & Atlantic Railroad. The Stanton House was built, the foundation of an immense opera-house was laid, a large railway station was erected, and that part of Market Street was thoroughly macadamized. For a time success crowned the effort; and then came the big fire in 1870, which swept away the "shanties and shebangs" along the west side of Market. At the same time the Alabama & Chattanooga Railway Company failed, and with it failed the scheme for removal. The Stanton House remains, but the opera-house foundation is occupied by a freight-house, and the great wooden station-house has long since been pulled down.. The "shanties and shebangs" were gradually supplanted by handsome brick stores.

Not until the eighties was the future of Chattanooga assured beyond the possibilities. In 1887 there came a marvellous wave of prosperity. To be sure it had its exaggerations and some unhealthiness, but progress has been continuous ever since. Now we are indeed assuming metropolitan airs. We have all the conveniences of advanced civilization, and all the appliances necessary to build up a solid, healthful, beautiful city. Our location has wrought wonders in our behalf.

Ex-Mayor Hewitt, of New York City, made this city a visit in April last, and predicted that a million and a half of people would occupy these valleys and swarm upon their mountain walls long before the close of the twentieth century. Mr. Jay Gould expressed the opinion, while standing on the "Point" last winter, that we would have one hundred thousand souls before the close of nineteen hundred.

The negro problem is creating some anxiety among thoughtful citizens, but the influx of Americans from the North, and of foreigners from Germany and Ireland, will solve that problem. The writer will not live to see the pressing southward of that unfortunate race by this invasion from the north and from beyond seas. But the negro has been pressed southward from New England, and his destiny is as assuredly southward as was the Indian's destiny westward. Within fifty years the negro will be as infrequent in the valleys of Chattanooga and Lookout as he now is in the valley of the Gennessee in New York.

Chattanooga is thoroughly cosmopolitan. All good people who desire to make an honest living are sought after. The gates of the city swing inward to welcome all such, for the commingling of the blood of northerner and southerner will produce the most vigorous race known to the annals of humanity. Such a race will have but one Law, one Union, one God!

THE CLIMATE.

Most important of all attractions to persons seeking a desirable place of residence is the climate of Chattanooga. Think of a spot where it is cool in summer and warm in winter—the mountain walls that ward off the winter's chilly blasts from the north form funnels, through which the gentle breezes in summer from the southwest sweep through the valley by day, and especially by night. This condition of natural surroundings makes the heat from the sun bearable by day and the rest at night sweet and refreshing in summer. In winter the mountains and ridges fold their arms around the city and protect it from the cruel blasts of what the white flags, with black squares in the center, represent as cold waves.

A prominent physician, who came to this city from his home in Massachusetts because of lung troubles, said this in a public lecture:

"Who among us is not mindful of the rich delights of our usual March climate? March! that month of terror in other latitudes, brings us the blossoms of spring in rich profusion, the working days in our gardens and flower-beds, and gives us a noonday warmth of 80 degrees, while the coolness of night rarely causes the mercury to fall to 40. April follows with its luxuriant wealth of flowers in field, forests, and lawn; the rich and varied verdure of the mountain slopes; the grand picnic days; the profusion of blossoming laurel and azalea; the time when we feel most the exhilaration of a tonic atmosphere, and youth comes again to age. And then follows May. Beautiful! beautiful! glorious May! Who can describe an East Tennessee May in any other way than by exclamations? May flowers! No indeed. We squander those in March. We hurry past our roses of the commoner sorts in April, and come into realization of the complete bliss of living in the real native land of the continual blossoming rose, in the early days of May, when the black boys peddle young mocking-birds through the streets, and the luscious red strawberries come, so sweet, so plenty and so welcome. And then comes June. Young summer, older than May, wiser, larger, fuller, and bringing the first harvests of ripened grain; holding in its provident lap the most liberal bestowals of the Almighty in rewards for the labors of man, with a great bonus of earth's spontaneous fruits. And there are no hot days yet. No sweltering nights.

"Can a better summer resort be pictured? If consumptives want altitude and mild climate together, and upon that all authorities agree, it is to be found here. These mountains are so common to us, who use them for daily, weekly and monthly convenience in the summer days, a sleeping place away from the dust and mosquitoes, as well as cooler home quarters, that we have no just appreciation of them. But the mountains of East Tennessee are destined to occupy a high place in the public estimation, in future, as a living place for invalids."

Another physician, who also came here from the North, has this to say of our surrounding mountains:

"During the last six years I have spent the summers on Walden's Ridge. I speak of what I have seen with my own eyes, and know to be true, that if tubercles are not already formed on the lungs, and continue fully developed within the body of the lungs, a residence of a year, yea, even sometimes a few months, will dispel all fears of a consumptive death from the mind of the unfortunate. I know that I have seen them carried up the ridge apparently in the last stages of phthisic, coughing incessantly, and yet they lived for months, slowly improving every day, until, thinking they were nearly well, they left the mountain, went back to the Northern clime, and in a few weeks the inevitable occurred. I have visited nearly every house on Walden's Ridge, every cabin and hut, and I have rarely seen a native with any lung trouble whatever.

"I could almost say the same of Sand Mountain, Lookout Mountain and divers other places, did time permit.

"We, fortunately, are living in a clime midway between the icy regions of the North and the hot, sultry air of the South—a spot where it is not too warm for comfort, not too cold to even bundle up on the coldest of days; certainly the most healthy, the most pleasant clime known to me on earth. Adopting Chattanooga as my home in 1865, I say it, without fear of contradiction, that we have the most healthy climate, the most prosperous city, the most pleasant and hospitable people that the sun shines on. May the balance of my life be spent among them, for verily my lines have been cast in pleasant places."

It may be of interest to those who determine the balminess of a city by the general direction of the winds to say that the prevailing direction of wind at Chattanooga is southwest, at St. Louis south, at Cincinnati southeast, at Toledo southwest, at Albany south, at Washington west, at Omaha south, and Pittsburg northwest.

EDUCATIONAL FACILITIES.

The Public School System of Chattanooga is an admirable one, patterned after the best models, and conducted in the most practical, satisfactory manner. There is a Board of Education, sixteen members, and a Superintendent, sixty-

2

four teachers, five Primary Schools, four Grammar Schools, and two High Schools. These are conducted in six large, convenient, well heated and ventilated, and thoroughly drained buildings.

There are four grades in the Primary Schools, four grades in the Grammar Schools, and three classes, junior, middle and senior, in the High Schools.

LOCATION OF SCHOOL BUILDINGS.

CHATTANOOGA HIGH SCHOOL, corner of Gillespie and Early streets.

HOWARD HIGH SCHOOL, Gilmer street.

FIRST DISTRICT, corner McCallie avenue and Douglas street.

SECOND DISTRICT, corner of Gillespie and Early streets.

THIRD DISTRICT. William street.

GILMER STREET SCHOOL, Gilmer street.

MONTGOMERY AVENUE SCHOOL, Montgomery avenue.

There are a number of private schools, which are made necessary by the views of their patrons. These schools are reported to be conducted to the entire satisfaction of those patrons.

NOTRE DAME DE LOUDRES ACADEMY.

This School, under control of the Catholic Church, is conducted by the Dominican Sisters. The building is large, conveniently arranged for its purposes, and there are praises only for the charming, uniformed women who conduct it. It is a parochial school, as well as a young ladies' seminary, and the building stands on the Catholic Church square.

We hazard nothing in affirming that the educational facilities of Chattanooga (see "Chattanooga University," page 29) are all that can be desired, and this opinion is continually being confirmed by families removing to this city to secure the thorough education of their children.

Not only are the Public School buildings for the separate education of whites and blacks ample and commodious, they are handsome from an architectural standpoint, and healthful. The colored people are as amply provided for as are the whites. Their teachers are of their own race, without exception.

THE CHURCHES.

Chattanoogans, with pardonable pride, point out to visitors their handsome church edifices. The Methodist Episcopal Church, corner of McCallie and Georgia avenues, is of blue limestone, and surmounted by a lofty spire. Its windows attract special attention. Near by, on Gilmer street, the Methodist Episcopal Church, South, is of brick, its tall, graceful spire visible from all points in the valley. On the same street, and near to Georgia avenue, is the immense Catholic Church building, flanked by the home of the Dominican Sisters, who teach in the large school building close by, and by the pastor's house, on Georgia avenue. The First Baptist Church has a massive building, on Georgia avenue, built of pink sandstone, with drab facings, the windows of which are wonderfully beautiful; and on the same avenue, corner of Seventh, is the brick structure of the First Presbyterian Church. Close by, on Walnut street, is the tasty, modestly trimmed Church of the Christians; and on Oak street you see the delicate spire of the Cumberland Presbyterian Church.

On the West side of Market, corner of Eighth and Chestnut, is the present edifice of the Second Presbyterian Church. This church is preparing to build a handsome house of worship.

On the corner of Pine and Seventh is the immense pile known as St. Paul's Protestant Episcopal Church. The Rectory and Parochial School are included in this pile.

The colored people have erected two handsome church buildings—one by the Baptists, on Gilmer, the other by the Methodists, on corner of Lookout and Fifth streets.

The Jewish Synagogue is on Walnut street, and is soon to be remodeled and beautified.

These are the main edifices, but there are quite a number of less expensive buildings in different parts of the city and in the suburbs. The Unitarians worship in the Hall of the Chamber of Commerce, but announce their intention of erecting a house of worship next year.

THE RAILROADS.

Not only has Chattanooga a great waterway for the movement of raw material that does not demand rapid transportation, but it is the terminus of eight trunk railways, that are not only well equipped, but are provided with ample terminal facilities.

The Western & Atlantic was the first railway to enter the valley; it was built by the State of Georgia. In the early days of its business, cotton bales were wont to be piled the entire length of Mulberry (now Broad) street, from the river to the railway's freight shed, at Ninth street, awaiting transportation. Then the locomotives and freight cars were but toys in comparison to those of the present day, and complaints of shippers were loud and fierce. The city gave this road a right of way down Mulberry to the river, and that right was not surrendered until 1872. Mulberry street was widened from 60 to 126 feet for the uses of the railroad, and its name was changed to Railroad avenue. This will yet be the main thoroughfare.

The Nashville & Chattanooga road came next after the Western & Atlantic, and gave access to the rich granaries of Middle Tennessee, and also provided a continuous rail from the future capital of Georgia to the capital of Tennessee. This stimulated the building of the Louisville & Nashville.

The East Tennessee did not at first extend the main line any further than Cleveland, and built a branch to Dalton, Ga., to make connection with the Western & Atlantic, and supply the South with the surplus of cereals and meat found in East Tennessee. Several years after the opening to Dalton the main line was built into Chattanooga, piercing Missionary Ridge with a tunnel instead of going around its northern extremity, as the Western & Atlantic had done. This road has since built a line from Chattanooga to Atlanta and Macon, connecting with its road to Brunswick, on the lower Atlantic.

The Wills Valley Railroad, which was surveyed to Meridian, Miss., in 1847, was running to Trenton, Ga., when the war began. After the war it was completed to Meridian and called the Alabama & Chattanooga. Subsequently it was bought by the present owners and the name changed to Alabama Great Southern.

The Memphis & Charleston, whose rails end at Stephenson, Ala., and whose connections with the East Tennessee system at Chattanooga are made over the rails of the Nashville & Chattanooga, was the great East & West line when the war began. Its name implies a through rail connection of the Father of Waters with the broad Atlantic, through Chattanooga, Atlanta, Augusta and Charleston.

The city of Cincinnati, in full appreciation of its southern trade, built the great Cincinnati Southern through the mountains of Tennessee, boring thirteen tunnels through its ridges, at an expense of over twenty millions of dollars. The owners of the Alabama Great Southern are the lessees of this highway. This and the Louisville & Nashville are competitors for the freights that pass to and through Chattanooga.

The Chattanooga, Rome & Columbus is a new line, opening up a country of great importance to Chattanooga. It passes the battle-field of Chickamauga, and crosses close to Crawfish Spring, over the river that flows out of that spring.

The Union (or Belt) Railway surrounds the city, and sends out branches to the various suburbs. It has created and maintained those suburbs by low rates and quick service, both of passengers and freights.

Several railroads are projected—one to Augusta, Ga., another to connect with the North Carolina system via Murphy, and a local road to the summit of Walden's Ridge, and Signal Point; the latter the rival of the Point of Lookout. It is also believed that the Memphis & Charleston will extend its rails into Chattanooga through South Pittsburg and Sequachee Valley, crossing the Tennessee at Chattanooga. When this is done, and the bridge is completed over the river, "Hill City" will become the most populous of the suburbs.

The railroads have *made* Chattanooga. The chronic war that always exists between railways and cities has not escaped Chattanooga for all that. Hence, the citizens are looking for the completion of the Muscle Shoals Canal with more than ordinary anxiety. They expect to use the river as a liquid club with which to frighten the railways into lower and more equitable rates of freight. But, club or no club, the railroads will remain the great arteries through which will come and go the life blood of Chattanooga.

The roads to the summit of Lookout were completed in 1887 and in 1889, and are described in the Excursions. They have done much for the comfort of our citizens by furnishing rapid transit during the warm months of summer. They have also added to the importance of the mountain by making its airy summit easy of access to excursionists and pleasure seekers.

The Electric Railway makes Missionary Ridge even more easy of access than

Lookout, and has added greatly to the comforts of the large population now living on that beautiful and historic hill-top.

Next in importance to the railroads is the great river, whose passage to the Mississippi has been interrupted by the Muscle Shoals. These obstructions and the necessity of removing them are not by any means new discoveries. More than fifty years ago the whole question was discussed by the ablest statesmen and engineers in the country, and it is probable that the pernicious doctrine which prevailed at that time, that the General Government ought not to engage in internal improvements, had a great deal to do with the smallness of the results.

A few facts will illustrate the importance of this waterway to Chattanooga:

The Tennessee is open all winter, at the very time when the Northern water routes are frozen up and the railroads are putting on the highest rates. For this reason boats from the Ohio River which are obliged to lay up for the winter, and are so much in danger of ice gorges that Congress has been considering the propriety of expending a large sum to build harbors of refuge for them, could afford to come down here during the winter and work for the lowest rates that would pay running expenses.

The Chattanooga coal and iron fields are 450 miles nearer the mouth of the Ohio River than is the city of Pittsburg, which amounts to saying that we have that distance the start of Pittsburg in reaching any point on the Mississippi, or its western tributaries. Chattanooga has about the same advantage, so far as distance is concerned, that she would have if Pittsburg were located above Bristol, Tenn., and had to run its freights down the river.

The assurance is given at this writing that before Christmas of 1889 steamboats will be passing freely through the Muscle Shoals Canal, and Chattanooga will have uninterrupted water transportation connection with the world.

A TOUR OF THE CITY.

Let us now conduct the visitor on a short tour of the city, and we will begin at the Union Passenger Depot. if he is willing to our guidance.

We drive down Market street, along the fine asphalt pavement, until we reach Fourth street, where stands the principal historical house of the city, the three-story, plain brick building on the southwest corner. It is now the city building, and is flanked by the city jail on the west. It is battered, bolted, and somewhat unshapely, for it was the first brick house erected in the city. It was built in 1840 of the bricks burned with the wood that was cleared off what are now Market and Broad streets, and the owners, Messrs. Whiteside, Williams & Bridgeman, were pronounced the most venturesome of men.

Drive over to Broad, along Fourth, and then up Broad to Seventh. Go west until you reach the large ecclesiastical pile known as the Protestant Episcopal Church. Take a peep at its unique interior, and then ascend to the summit of Cameron Hill by the road on the eastern brow. While you ascend, the prospect widens and brightens until the valley of Chattanooga, with its prosperous city, its bright painted suburbs, its forest of brick and iron smoke stacks, its great throbbing, rumbling factories, its iron highways, its historic mountain walls, its vineyards and orchards and majestic river lies beyond and behind you; a beautiful panorama, full of color, life and promise for the future.

The carriage will halt at the base of the now broken flag-staff, that was set up there in 1881, when the stars and stripes were run up to its lofty summit by a member of the Society of the Army of the Cumberland and a member of the specially-organized-for-the-occasion society of ex-Confederates. And when the grand old ensign flashed in the sun of that September day the cannons planted on demolished Fort Wood poured forth a salute that was echoed by the shouts of the thousands that swarmed upon Cameron Hill and upon the streets of the city below.

Descending from your carriage, you alight where stood a battery when Gen. Mitchell indulged the diversion one Sunday morning of shelling the city while the people were at prayer. Where you see the fine brick "Central Block," corner of Market and Seventh streets, there stood the Presbyterian Church, which was struck by one of those shells, and dismissed the congregation without a benediction.

Begin your examination of the panorama at the base of Mount Lookout, just where the "Point" stands out so clear-cut against the southwestern sky. The foliage of the Moccasin conceals the river as it sweeps around the base of the great obstruction to flow northward again toward the open gateway, which is seen beyond the heart-shaped island directly west. Raccoon Mountain, 1,000 feet above the gently flowing water, forms the western wall of the valley, and a pillar of the gateway to this valley of imperishable memories. It is only a few hundred yards across the "ankle" to where the tide is parted by an island just as it enters the mountain gorge, hurries on to the Father of Waters, and thence to the gulf.

Walden's Ridge, with its level plateau and precipitous bluffs, is dotted with summer houses. Between the river, above which you stand, and the base of this ridge, you can discover a well wooded stretch of land, on whose billowy bosom numerous white cottages nestle in the ample shade. A church steeple assures you of the permanancy of this suburb, now known as "Hill City," and the superb bridge, soon to be thrown over the river, will make it a favorite among the suburban claimants.

Below you see saw mills and planing mills and the rails of the Union Railway. On the rounded, detached terrace, on the eastern side of your point of observation, are the reservoirs of the water-works, now abandoned for the works described elsewhere.

Looking due east, and near to the river, you will discover the Confederate monument in the densely shaded "old cemetery"; also the stacks of the water-works and of Citico Blast Furnace. Turning a little to the right the floating ensign of the Union locates the beautifully kept enclosure of the National Cemetery. Beyond these is Missionary Ridge, and dotting the valley from Boyce to East Lake are the suburbs, better seen from the summit of Lookout.

RESIDENCE ON EAST FOURTH STREET.

You now see within the corporate limits the University and the spires of the two Methodist and the two Presbyterian churches, and also the towers of the Baptist and of the immense Catholic Church. The court-house, handsomely designed and honestly erected, stands in the open green beside the wooden Baptist church.

Having feasted your eyes on this attractive landscape, resume your carriage and begin the descent by the old roadway on the western side. The rocky "point" of Lookout is projected into the air, and to it you see the smoke and steam of factories ascending like incense—an offering of gratitude to that vigilant sentinel whose eyes never close in neglectful slumber.

Your carriage enters the western road at the spot where stood the catafalque, and where the Society of the Army of the Cumberland and the Society of ex-Confederates held memorial services on September 22, 1881, for the President of the United States, James A. Garfield, whose remains were then lying in state at the nation's capital. Surely that spot was made sacred by those tearful services.

We are unable to paint the scenes of that memorable day on Cameron Hill. On the extreme summit, which you have just left, and on the brow overlooking the Tennessee, had been reared the flag-staff, now gone to decay; and a garrison flag, heavily draped, lay with its halyards at the base of the pole. An immense multitude, representing every race and color that has sought an asylum in our great country, stood around, leaving only a small open space for the ceremonies. Along the slope, down to the canopied stand on which the orations were to be pronounced, stood the waiting thousands. The sun poured down its fierce meridian rays, unobscured by a single cloud, but there was not a murmur. Southward arose grand old Lookout, like a sentinel above the Moccasin Bend, and guarding the approach to the sacred spot where slept the brave men who made the distant fields of Missionary Ridge and Chickamauga immortal. Up from the city came the long procession of ex-Federal and ex-Confederate soldiers, their banners draped and drooping, and their bands playing solemn music. There was naught of gaud or display; it was a long funeral cortege, a tribute of love to him whose ashes lay in state at the capitol of the republic.

The canopied stand, heavily draped, had a large portrait of the martyred President suspended in the center. In front of the rostrum was an inclosure, in the center of which was a beautiful catafalque covered with white cloth and decorated with the choicest of cut-flower emblems, vines and evergreens. On the summit of that flowery pyramid an immense urn was surmounted by a floral cross and crown. This was the work of the ladies of Chattanooga, a committee of whom sat at its base during the ceremonies.

Soon the procession reached the hill-top and the base of the flag-staff. The marshals of both armies approached the staff and saluted. The two chiefs grasped the halyards, the band rent the air with the "Star Spangled Banner," the artillery at Fort Wood fired a salve of thirty-eight guns. Up went the old flag, the halyards moving under the hands of an ex-Federal and an ex-Confederate, and as the breeze caught up the graceful folds of that most beautiful of ensigns, the war-worn veterans went wild with delight. Cheer after cheer rent the air Then the band played "Dixie," and the enthusiasm arose almost to madness.

Men who once were enemics threw their hats into the air and rushed into each other's arms, and on the summit of Cameron Hill, in full view of Lookout, Mission Ridge and Chickamauga, and of the National and Confederate Cemeteries, the American Union was irrevocably restored beyond the disintegrating power of demagogue or madman.

Presently the thrilling notes of the band changed to a dirge. The flag slowly descended to half mast, hats were removed and a hush pervaded the multitude that a moment before was wild with excitement. Every eye was moist with tears of sympathy for the sweet, good woman who then sat by the bier of him the nation delighted to honor.

The procession returned to the rostrum, which was already packed with distinguished ex-Confederate and Federal officers. The space around the inclosure containing the catafalque was so densely packed that several fainted. When the procession occupied the space allowed them, there was not a green spot or Cameron Hill visible to the tallest man who stood upon the raised platform; it was covered with a mass of human beings, densely packed, and awaiting with bated breath the utterings of the Confederate welcome.

Following the addresses, made by S. A. Key for the Confederates and by J. W. Keifer for the Society of the Army of the Cumberland, came the reqniem services, led by Rev. J. W. Bachman, D. D., an ex-Confederate colonel. The music, the prayer, the Scriptures, the addresses, the sorrowing Templars and weeping women, were all in unison—a tribute of love to the martyred, and an expression of affection and sympathy for the bereaved widow and fatherless children. At its conclusion, the people silently descended the hill, and those who stood near the catafalque begged for the flowers and vines to carry home as sacred memorials of the tender occasion.

As you continue the descent, you see on the narrow strip of land between mount and river the planing mill of Hughes & Co., the electric light plant, the buildings of the Roane Iron Company's steel mill, and the plant of Montague & Co., where are made fire-bricks and vitrified sewer pipes in very large quantities.

Instruct your hackman to drive out Magazine street to Terrace, where you will find several of the handsomest residences of the city. The circuit of the Terrace is made around the elegant residence of Capt H. S. Chamberlain, and a good view is obtained of the Tannery plant of Fayerweather & Ladew, in the centre of which is securely sandwiched the lofty stack, cupola and outlying buildings of the Chattanooga Iron Company's blast furnace.

Admission to this Tannery, one of the largest in the world, is obtained at the office, and you are conducted over acres of concealed vats, in which lie thousands upon thousands of hides; on by the currying department, where scores of sable artists, with huge knives, raise a scent that *excells* attar of roses; through miles of leather, bark, leeches and drying-houses. You will see thousands of gallons of bark coffee, heaps of white hair suitable for the making of camel's hair shawls, thousands of cords of oak bark awaiting the embraces of the huge coffee mills; enormous sheds full of belt leather, and then the clever acting machinery that has made dismantled sad irons no longer a necessity to the shoemaker; the oiling and drying apparatus, and finally the loading of the completed stock for shipment to the hydraulic presses of New York. The "sight" repays a journey from New England.

If time permits, visit the Blast Furnace, examine its mighty blowers, its huge cupola, its seventy times heated "stoves," its batteries of boilers, its storing sheds for ore, coke and limestone. But most interesting is the making of a cast, when the molten iron rushes down a narrow channel, and is adroitly turned into the "sows," which feed the pigs on both sides, until thirty tons of the metal lies steaming in its beds of sand. And when the iron has all run out, the pyrotechnics that follow exceed anything possible to less ambitious appliances. It is believed by some that the attendants on such performances should hold a lively appreciation of the startling possibilities of a life of depravity.

Now take your carriage and drive out Montgomery avenue, noting the handsome public school building recently erected for colored children. You whirl over the smooth macadamized road until you reach the great stone gateway of the

NATIONAL CEMETERY.

As you approach the sacred enclosure the magnificent gateway looms up before you. It is built of Alabama limestone, with an archway 37 feet in height, in which swings a heavy iron gate. This gateway cost $17,000 by special contract. While you halt, as the gate turns on its hinges to allow you ingress, you will read the following inscription on the entablature:

NATIONAL MILITARY CEMETERY.

CHATTANOOGA, A. D., 1863.

Passing under the lofty arch, you again halt upon the beautiful white gravel, and, turning around, read on the inside entablature this inscription:

HERE REST IN PEACE 12,956 CITIZENS,

WHO DIED FOR THEIR COUNTRY

IN THE YEARS 1861 TO 1865.

You now drive slowly around the graveled walk, beside the dense and close-clipped osage hedge, which nearly conceals the well-coped wall that entirely surrounds the inclosure. The cemetery is circular, nearly one mile in circumference, and contains 75¼ acres. It was purchased at a cost of $15,000. In the centre rises a knoll fully 100 feet above the avenue on which you drive, and the grounds slope down to this exterior avenue in the most beautiful and undulating manner. It is well covered with blue-grass, which the diligent superintendent keeps closely shaven. On these verdant slopes are nineteen special interment sections, each marked by a small granite obelisk, and lettered A to S; and these are surrounded by the small white marble head and foot-stones. These sections are of different forms, in the arrangement of the graves, some forming triangles, others oblongs, others squares, others parallelograms, and others circles, while section E forms a shield.

Starting from the gateway and turning to your right, you will reach Section S., where are the private monuments of Major T. J. Carlile, Capt. B. S. Nicklin and wife, Capt. W. H. McDevitt, Capt. G. A. M. Estes and Dr. R. N. Barr.

Just above this is Section H., where, in a semi-circle, lie the ashes of the seven men who were hung for the capture of the passenger locomotive "General," at Big Shanty, on the Western & Atlantic Railroad, in 1862. You can leave your carriage and go on foot over the green sward to this section, and there you will find names on the headstones thus: Samuel Slovius, S. Robertson, G. D. Wilson, Marion Ross, W. Campbell, P. G. Shadrach, John Scott—all of Ohio.

On the 6th day of March, 1889, the Legislature of Ohio appropriated $5,000 for the erection of a monument to the memory of these brave men. We are told they were a picked company from a large number, each man being peculiarly fitted for certain railway work. One or more had been locomotive engineers, others were firemen, telegraphers, and each man knew just what duty he would be assigned to. The capture of the engine and the race from Big Shanty to the point near this city where they abandoned the engine and took to the woods and were captured and hung is well known history. They took their lives in their hands and they lost them.

The leader of this party, J. J. Andrews, was interred in this section on Sunday, October 16, 1887, with appropriate ceremonies. The writer of these lines was one of the military witnesses of the death of Andrews, and he hereby bears testimony that he died as does a fearless man.

You will continue (on foot) while your carriage drives around to meet you before the Superintendent's Lodge, till you reach the summit of the knoll. On this summit is the flag-staff, on which floats the Ensign of the Union, and the great brick rostrum of 40 x 20 feet area, 5 feet high, with handsome cut-stone coping and an interior carpet of velvety grass. An open roof of purloins and joists is supported by 12 square pillars, and these are covered with the ivy, woodbine and climbing vines so plentifully planted around the base.

Surrounding this rostrum is a close-shaven lawn, dotted with trees and shrubs, on which stand on end four immense cannous. One of these has the regulation shield, in bronze, on which is engraved, in raised letters:

UNITED STATES

NATIONAL MILITARY CEMETERY,

CHATTANOOGA.

ESTABLISHED. - 1863.

The cemetery was established under an order of General Thomas, issued December 25, 1863.

The records in the Superintendent's office give the following details:

First interment, February 18, 1863.

Officers..		204
White soldiers, known 6 804		
White soldiers, unknown............................4,943	—11,747	
Colored soldiers, known 885		
Colored soldiers, unknown.......................... 20—	905	
Civilians		154

Total interments to May 15, 1889   13,010

The only large monument in the cemetery is the one erected to the Dead of the 4th Army Corps, and is a handsome marble obelisk, rising from a plinth properly inscribed on all sides. There are several private monuments. One in Section C to Lieut.-Col. J. B. Taft, of New York, and one in Section F to Dr. A. L. Cox, of the 20th Corps. In Section E is one to Maj. S. F. McKeehan, of Indiana, and one to Lieut. Adam Lowry, of Pennsylvania. In Section A is a monument to Capt. J. H. Lereve, of Indiana; one to Col. G. de Mihalotzy, of Illinois, and one to Capt. W. C. Russell, A. A. G. In Section D is a monument to Capt. J. Gnnsenhouser, of Indiana.

The following is a

RECAPITULATION

By States of the interments:

United States Regulars......	203	Missouri	168
Alabama	38	New Jersey..................	32
Connecticut.....	20	New York..................	346
Georgia......................	11	Ohio	1,823
Illinois	1.103	Pennsylvania	198
Indiana.....................	1 338	Rhode Island	2
Iowa	187	Tennessee	133
Kansas	58	Wisconsin	238
Kentucky...................	369	West Virginia....	3
Maryland	2	Pioneers.....................	5
Maine	1	Signal Corps	3
Massachusetts...............	73	Employes...................	14
Michigan	489	Miscellaneous..............	5,018
Minnesota	107	Colored.....................	885

The Government built the macadamized road from Montgomery avenue to the Cemetery gate. This is thirty feet wide. The right of way is 80 feet wide, and shade trees will be planted on both sides the entire distance. It is a pity that this drive is somewhat neglected.

The total expense of the Cemetery up to January 1, 1889, was $215,000 in round numbers. It is now the second National Cemetery in point of beauty, and if improvements continue it will soon be second to none.

No visitor to Chattanooga should fail to include this lovely City of the Dead in excursions. Its beautiful lawn, shade trees and flowering shrubs, its roses and trailing vines, make it all that affection and patriotism could desire. It is sad to remember that thirteen thousand brave men sleep beneath this emerald carpet, but the patriot finds consolation in the memory that they died for their country.

After registering at the Superintendent's lodge, you will resume your carriage. Passing under the archway again you are driven to the elevated site known as Fort Wood, near which stand the huge filters of the water-works. There, amid piles of material for the building of the residences going up all around, you have a very effective view of the valley of Chattanooga.

From Fort Wood you drive to the

CHATTANOOGA UNIVERSITY,

an imposing stucture, which is easily discovered from the cars of each of the railways that enter the city. It is the educational building erected by the

Methodist Episcopal Church, whose beautiful house of worship is at the western terminus of McCallie avenue.   This institution was chartered July 9, 1886, and the main building was completed September 16, 1886.   The first term began on September 15th.   It has a full corps of teachers, and four schools are organized: Academic, Collegiate and Art.   There is a good library and good apparatus. This school was consolidated with the one at Athens in 1889, and is now known as the "Grant Memorial University."   The real estate and endowments of these consolidated schools are put down at $500,000.   "The University is not operated for financial profit, and uses its large revenues in reducing the cost of an education to students."

The two-story brick building west of the campus is the "Central High School" of the city system of public schools.   It is more commodious than beautiful.

You can now drive down the northern slope of the college eminence and visit the

CONFEDERATE CEMETERY.

There lie thousands of those who wore the gray, beneath the shade of weeping willows, with graves unmarked, while a monument, with a shaft thirty feet in height, stands on the highest spot in the enclosure, bearing the simple inscription, "Our Confederate Dead." Mrs. G. C. Connor was president of the association of ladies who built it, and Mr. W. D. VanDyke was their treasurer. Maj. G. C. Connor was the designer of the monument. United States troops, with Capt. Cochran at their head, entered this cemetery with reversed arms, the band of his regiment (Col. Wheaton's) preceding them, and participated in the laying of the corner-stone, which was laid by Hon. Jas. D. Richardson, then Grand Master of Freemasons, and now member of Congress. The larger portion of the fund that reared this monument was contributed by Northern-born residents of Chattanooga. Such is the spirit that has animated our people since 1870. Such is the spirit that animates the entire South to-day.

> Blot out the lines that would divide
> And desecrate our sod ;
> Bind close our States, give us one law,
> One Union and one God.

And may we not hope that that spirit will spread until it animates the entire nation, and its government shall recognize in these brave defenders of their principles gallant citizens of the United States. The grassy, shaded necropolis is indeed a sacred memory of American valor.

From the Confederate Cemetery you drive to your hotel along Vine street, passing the Orphans' Home, the brilliant edifice of the First Baptist Church and the court-house. When driving down Seventh you will turn into Market street. You soon reach the

UNION PASSENGER DEPOT.

All travelers admire this handsome depot, into which most of the railways run their trains. It contains two waiting-rooms and a ladies' parlor, baggage-room, telegraph office, ticket office, dining-room, lunch-stand, kitchen, and seven handsome offices up stairs. The seatings are solid walnut, elegantly finished. The mantels are slate and marble, and the chandeliers of modern designs. Electric lamps, in addition to the gas, illuminate the building. The main corridor is paved with Georgia marble. The front is of Zanesville pressed brick, with black cut joints, and a fine clock decorates the cupola. Two grass plats, surrounded by a massive curbing and pavement, lie between its front and the street. All the conveniences are well up to the demands of the times, and the city, as well as the railways, are justly proud of it.

Should you stop at the Stanton, you will go up Ninth street from the Union Depot and pass the place where the Government is erecting the Custom-house on "Stone Fort," a lofty site, with solid rock foundation. You will reach en route the

CENTRAL RAILWAY STATION.

This spacious depot was erected by the Cincinnati, New Orleans & Texas Pacific Railway Company. In addition to the arrival and departure of their own

trains, those of the East Tennessee, Virginia & Georgia, of the Memphis &
Charleston, and of the Chattanooga, Rome & Columbus stop there on their
way in and out of the city.   The open train shed is supplemented by handsome
waiting-rooms, lunch-stand and all modern comforts.

You are now ready for dinner, and there are three first-class hotels, that are
supplemented by a large number of smaller ones, in which you can obtain it.   A
tour of the Industries may be made after you are refreshed.

EXCURSIONS TO LOOKOUT MOUNTAIN.

There are three routes to the Summit of historic Lookout—one, the oldest, by carriage up the well-kept St. Elmo Turnpike, another up the standard gauge "Lookout Mountain Railroad," and the other up the "Incline"—and along the Narrow Gauge to Sunset Rock.

1. BY CARRIAGE UP ST. ELMO TURNPIKE.

Taking your carriage early in the morning, you will drive out Whiteside street, by the murky stacks of Lookout Rolling Mill, the Stove and the Pipe Works, and in full view of the busy valley and its hundred factories, crossing on the tall iron bridge over Chattanooga Creek, while you gaze at the projecting mass called the "Point," now clearly defined against the western sky.

Having reached the foot of the mountain, you begin the ascent of the St. Elmo road. You drive by easy grades to the bluff overlooking Cascade Glen; then you descend to the bridge that crosses the brook, dashing along its rocky, precipitous bottom to the valley beyond. The ascent grows steeper over the remainder of the road, while passing in full view of the glen, every foot of which reveals new beauties and wonders. When you reach the summit you debouch on the regular mountain road. Then you look back into the glen, and gaze on its silvery brook, rushing over abrupt precipices, winding around immense bowlders, or singing along over its pebbly bottom till it is lost in the dense foliage beyond the bridge. On either side the precipitous mountains close in the view, and on a spur which projects into the glen, on the south side, you catch a glimpse of the old United States Hospital, on its lofty perch, and exclaim, as thousands have done before, "What a lovely spot for a hotel."

Having reached the summit, you instruct the driver to turn his horses toward Rock City. The drive is not as smooth as a boulevard, but its very ruggedness adds to your enjoyment of the scenery. You dash along between the trees, when suddenly you are in full view of the ruins of the immense wooden buildings erected for a hospital by General Thomas, in 1864-5, at a cost of $285,000, when General King was encamped with the 15th, 16th, 18th and 19th regulars on the camp ground west of Rock City, and through the ruined chimneys of which you will pass en route to Lulu Lake. At the close of the war these buildings were purchased by the philanthropist, Mr. Robert, and used as a school for boys and girls. The venture proved a failure, and the school was closed. Then the buildings were removed, little by little, until scarcely any remain.

Having passed over the branch of Cascade Glen, and ascended to the ridge on which stood this big building, you turn to the left into an almost abandoned road that leads you to the northern entrance of

ROCK VILLAGE.

You descend from your carriage and walk through a stone gateway that is formed by two rocks sixty feet high and fifty feet apart, each surmounted by a

3

cone resembling a sentinel. Stopping a moment at the round-table, you pass under the broken arch, leaving the "Witches Grotto," on your left, and presently you are in the "Coliseum," its massive ruins lying about in endless confusion. Your carriage has gone around by the highlands, and awaits you in the "suburbs."

You now stroll down the graveled walk and halt at Payne's Spring, gushing from a square opening in the rock, and taste its cool, freestone water. Then you walk around some more "ruins," and turn to the "Point," from which you can look up Payne's Ravine, on the left, its rocky walls pierced by numerous caves. On your right, the beautiful valley, hundreds of feet below, tempts you to descend to its green shadiness. Returning, you pass between the "Sisters" and the immense conglomerate, perched on one leg, called the "Pedestal." Here you see the "Ostrich Egg," which some fool soldiers overturned during the war, and just beyond is the immense mass called "Elephant Rock."

Avoiding the prickly cactus, which pierce your gloves and hands if you touch them, and feasting your eyes on the exquisite mosses, ferns and lichens, you bid adieu to the suburbs of Rock Village, re-enter your carriage, and drive over to

ROCK CITY.

A short walk between the trees brings you to the "Grand Corridor," the walls of which exclude the rays of the sun. You enter the narrow streets, whose mighty walls are conglomerate, and which are washed entirely smooth, rising sixty feet in height, and in many cases closing to less than a foot's distance apart.

One street leads up to the "Fat Man's Misery," a narrow and precipitous pass to the summit of the rocky battlements. If unable to ascend this pass, you can return and go around by the path you entered; but if you are small and spry enough to ascend there, you can walk along the battlements, jumping over the deep crevices between there and "Rock City Bluff." This is the wildest view on the mountain, overlooking the valley of Chattanooga, hundreds of feet below. It gives you a glimpse of the battle-fields of Chickamauga and Missionary Ridge, and an excellent view of Chattanooga and of the Tennessee River.

After testing the seats and niches of this bluff, you can visit the "Smoking Parlor," which is formed by an overhanging rock, with convenient seats scattered about. You next descend to "Rock City Avenue" through a narrow gateway, and find the street covered with loam, well shaded with elms and poplars, streams crossing it at various points, while narrow streets from other parts of the city come in through its tall conglomerate walls in a number of places. This is a favorite resort for picnic parties, being cool, well shaded, and supplied with delicious water. About one hundred yards from its southern entrance is the "Anvil Rock."

From this southern entrance you can drive to Chickamauga Bluff (a mile away), over which pours a stream of crystal water one hundred and fifty feet perpendicular, and from which point you can see distant Eagle Cliff, and Lulu Falls, the latter gleaming in the sunlight like a ribbon of silver.

You may now drive back by Rock City and out between the ruins of the chimneys of the Camping Ground, and turn your horses toward Lulu Lake. Take the upper, or right-hand road, which is a very fair mountain highway. You pass the "Georgia Chalybeate Springs," and soon after passing "Two Mile Tree" you reach Jackson's Hill, where charming glimpses are obtained of the Chattanooga and Lookout valleys on either side, and the white walls of the buildings around ancient Summer Town. In front you behold lofty High Point and Rising Fawn Bluff, resembling a cross range of mountains. Over "rough and rugged ways" you continue until at last you reach

LULA LAKE AND WOODBINE FALLS.

Quitting your carriage at the site of a once popular refreshment booth, you will descend to the rocky banks of Rock Creek, which pours down through lofty ledges, between mountains rising up into the clouds, and halt at Woodbine Falls, a sloping ledge, about thirty feet high, down which the brook pours into the blue waters of the circular basin called Lulu Lake. In spring the woodbine and honeysuckle bloom here in great profusion. You walk carefully along the northern ledge until you reach a projecting cliff of the stone wall, that looks down upon the stream, three hundred feet below. Here you take a rocky seat

SADDLE ROCK.

and feast your eyes on the sublime scene. Just above is the little brook pouring down Woodbine Falls into a circular basin resembling an inverted washbowl, about two hundred feet in circumference, and over fifty feet deep. After caressing the crystal lakelet, this scurrying brook escapes from the east side, rushes along a shelving channel and pours over a tall, curved precipice in silvery whiteness, forming the beautiful Lulu Falls, which you saw from Chickamauga Bluff. On the left are Chickamauga Bluff and Eagle Cliff, and the valley of Chickamauga is seen through the wildest of ravines, that begins at your feet.

Many prefer to cross the brook above Woodbine Falls and follow the pathway around the lake and the point to the base of the falls. Such can enter beneath the falls a capacious cavern, an exceedingly refreshing spot on a summer's day.

After feasting your eyes on this wild, weird scene, you resume your carriage and turn homewards. Having reached the road that leads to the "Natural Bridge" you will drive there at once.

The "Natural Bridge" property belongs to the Spiritualists, who have erected there an amphitheatre in which to hold their summer conventions. The "Bridge," the "Old Man of the Mountain" and the "Telephone Rock" are attractious and worthy of a visit.

From the "Natural Bridge" you can walk over to the Broad Gauge Railroad and ride down to the park, or you can continue on with your carriage to the southern terminus of the Narrow Gauge, just above Sunset Rock.

2. BY THE STANDARD GAUGE RAILROAD.

You will go to the Union depot and board a train of the Union, or Belt, Railroad early in the morning if you desire to make the entire tour of the mountain. It will be prudent, if you intend visiting the "city" and the lake, to telephone from your hotel to have a carriage in waiting when your train arrives at the Lookout Mountain House on the summit.

You will be comfortably conveyed through the valley, and by the pretty suburb, St. Elmo, and delivered at Mountain Junction in twenty minutes. There a climbing locomotive, equipped with all the appliances of strength and safety—things so necessary to mountain climbing—will seize hold of your coach and dash away with it up the bosom of the lofty hill at a speed of twenty miles an hour. The ascent is thrilling. First, a glimpse of St. Elmo, then a look of a few minutes' duration at that solemnly beautiful city of the dead, called Forest Hills; presently a vision of the valley, and of its suburbs leaning against Missionary Ridge, and then Chattanooga, reaching out to possess the land, which the broad, gently flowing river has limited only for a season.

Up and up and up races the iron horse, until he dashes into the field of the "Battle Above the Clouds." There it shrieks a halt, and cutting loose hurries to the rear of your coach. Again it ascends, but in the opposite direction, and its speed is not slackened. The galleried "Point Hotel" hangs out threateningly upon a terrace 200 feet above, and the sheer precipices frown their disapprobation of this noisy intrusion. Their immensity fills you with awe. The ladies on the galleries of the summer cottages, on the lower terrace, more hospitable than the beetling cliffs, wave their welcome to these lofty eyries with handkerchiefs and veils. And while you return the salutations the train dashes under the trestle of the "Incline" and speeds upward with quick pulsations until it rounds the bluff where stands "Lookout Mountain House" and its smiling cottages. The giant halts and you may alight.

You will now repair to the hotel and secure your carriage, as aforesaid, if you intend visiting Rock City and Lulu Lake. But before starting walk over to the bluff, on which stands a pretty summer-house. There you have a charming view of the valley, with the low line of Missionary Ridge on the east, and of the silvery river laving the feet of the city towards the north. Beyond Missionary Ridge are the foot hills that recall Chickamauga.

On this spot is frequently seen a remarkable phenomenon at sunrise. The valley is then filled up with a dense fog, entirely concealing it and the city, though not reaching quite up to the level of your point of observation. The sun, rising over Missionary Ridge, gives the white mist the appearance of the ocean, its waves rolling over the ridges, while the higher peaks of the foot hills loom up like islands in an Archipelago. The scene is indescribably lovely.

In the afternoons of summers there are other visions of loveliness, and which are never seen outside of such environments. Seated on this bluff you will frequently discover wreaths of vapor gracefully ascending here and there in the sunshine, to be kissed by cooling breezes, and descend in showers of pearls. The writer has counted as many as fifteen of those sunshine showers falling at one time in the valley beneath you, each shower bedewing an area of only a few hundred yards. The rainbow effects which sometimes accompany these showers are like those that were known to Solomon, when he said, "It compasseth the heaven about with a glorious circle, and the hands of the Most High have bended it." He who would attempt to paint such beauty must first dip his brush in dyes of heaven.

To visit Rock City and Lulu Lake follow the directions given in Route No. 1. But if you do not wish to drive there you can stroll along the brow of the mountain, or go over to the "Natural Bridge House" on foot.

If you do not alight from the train at Lookout Mountain House your train will whirl you over a tall trestle, beyond the Natural Bridge House, with its cottages and amphitheater, until the site of the park is reached, in which they are erecting a magnificent hotel.

From the park station you go on foot to the "Point." Do not halt at "Rock Bluff"; it will mar the effects of the vision at the "Point." Neither should you stop to climb "Observation Rock," or insist upon having a glimpse from "Signal Rock." Do not indulge more than a glance at curious "Umbrella Rock," but rush right down to the "Point." There you will be entranced.

And before we speak of the "Point" let us inhale a fragrant breath of these glorious mountains. Surely the prophecy of the wrapt Isaiah is here fulfilled: Yea, verily, the mountains and the hills break forth into singing, and all the trees of the valley do clap their hands for joy. These lofty hills raise their voices to the heavens, while the vales around, with their groves and streams, and human life, resound the notes, and "Let us worship God," they say with solemn sound.

447932

"THE POINT."

Nothing short of the divinely imparted descriptive afflatus is sufficient now. The view is unobstructed—beautiful, sublime. Down from the mountains of East Tennessee, North Carolina and Virginia flows the broad Tennessee, gleaming in silvery whiteness through the purple haze that hangs over the hills, and lovingly entering the valley that lies at your feet. The piers of the Cincinnati railway bridge show you where Sherman crossed that river and scaled the heights the morning of the battle of Missionary Ridge. Beyond the flag that floats above the National City of the Dead is Orchard Knob, the headquarters of Grant,

RICHARDSON BUILDING.

and on the Ridge, due east of where you stand, a lone tree marks the site of the headquarters of Bragg. What memories these historic spots recall!

In front of your lofty observatory is "Moccasin Bend," which the river has formed from the tongue of land that separates Chattanooga from the ridges on the west. Note the toe, the heel, the ankle, the almost perfect image of the Indian shoe. In the early summer the fields of waving grain, interspersed with patches of meadow and shade, give impressions of a beautiful garden, fenced with silver, and guarded from rude approach of storms by forest-clad hills just above the ankle. Many a lady has exclaimed, "It is an exquisite crazy quilt," and not a few masculines have poetically declared, "It is Eden."

Between you and the city, which spreads out around the base of Cameron Hill—its avenues and public buildings plainly visible, its very house signs being easily read with a glass—is the manufacturing district, the smoke of whose factories form a veil over the houses of the operatives. Ah! there is the source of Chattanooga's prosperity, and we will go with you to these factories to-morrow. Let us further scan the landscape.

On the northern extremity of Missionary Ridge we can detect among the heavy foliage the cottages and church spire of "Sherman Heights," the farthest away of our suburbs. Just a little beyond, at the base, is the village of Boyce, the junction of the Cincinnati Southern and the Western & Atlantic Railways. Nearer in are the cottages of "Stanley Town," a suburb set apart to colored people exclusively. Foaming up on the bosom of the ridge is the pretty suburb of Ridgedale, and as you peer through the haze, just over the beetling cliff beyond the photograph gallery you catch a glimpse of pretty East Lake, Chattanooga's favorite valley resort in the summer. Perhaps your eye can follow the train of the Union Railway as it winds around the lake on its way back to the city.

No pen, no matter how deeply dipped in romance, poetry and imagination, can describe the landscape you now behold. Nor is it in limner's power to transfer to canvas this prospect of hills and vales, of streams and lawns, of spires and factories, for the scene is ever changing, ever new; and with its shading of sun and cloud never like what it was an hour before. There are loftier mountains, more sublime stretches of precipice and beetling cliff, taller peaks and deeper gorges, but there is no spot on this western world where beauty is so charmingly united to sublimity, and where one's soul is so thrilled without being awed by appalling surroundings.

Glance at the two pretty streams that bend and curve through the valleys on each side of you and empty their excess of fructifying blessings into the river in front; look away beyond Sunset Rock to the last of the Appalachian hills vanishing on the plains of Alabama, and then look up to the great plateau of the Cumberland, where is established the University of the South, and the Southern Chautauqua—Monteagle. This mountain wall divides Tennessee into Eastern and Middle. Turn around, and the mountains you see away to the north and east are in Virginia, the Carolinas and Georgia. Directly eastward, and beyond Missionary Ridge, are the mountains that bound the battle-field of Chickamauga and through which Sherman marched and fought to Atlanta. Five States compose this glorious panorama.

VIEW NEAR CHATTANOOGA.

On the west the mountain wall is pierced by a gateway, through which the Tennessee flows out of this valley on its way to the sea. Reluctantly does this mountain give it passage, for the broken edges of the chasm abut right on the water's edge for miles. And the river itself appears to leave with equal reluctance, while it forms an island-heart as a symbol of its affection for the vale it is leaving. And ever and anon this seemingly gentle stream rises up to emphasize its affection for the enchanted valley, by embracing the lowlands and bathing the dusty feet of the highlands. Thousands annually reciprocate this affection by floating on its placid bosom, in excursions, through the exquisite scenery its channel has created.

While you gaze on all this loveliness you can scarcely be persuaded that twenty-five years ago these now peaceful valleys were filled with armed men, thirsting for each others blood; and that up the slope of that mountain where now are white houses, orchards and vineyards, these same armed men rushed through a storm of iron hail. But the emerald green knoll over yonder, with wall and massive gateway, and dotted with specks of white marble, tell the story of those terrible days. And that melancholy story is continued in another green spot, shaded by elms and willows, near the bank of the river. There the heroes of the blue and the grey await the resurrection trump.

Leaving the "Point," you take the pathway that leads by the "Umbrella" to the stairs that descend from Roper's Rock. Descending these steps and the rugged pathway you quickly reach the platform of the Narrow Gauge Railway, and the lower gallery of Lookout Point Hotel. From this platform you will take the train for

SUNSET ROCK.

Lookout Valley, with its green fields, white houses, meandering brooks and iron highways, is in full view from the windows of your car. The Tennessee disappears just as a locomotive screams good-bye while the train hurries away into Alabama.

Soon you reach the Rock, which is projected boldly out from the mountain, and on which a photograph gallery is securely anchored. From this point, in mid-air, the Confederates watched the Federals manœuvering for the relief of the garrison of Chattanooga. And here is frequently seen as brilliant sunsets as occur in any part of the world. In certain kinds of weather the vision of the god of day descending beyond lofty Cumberland, to lay aside his robes, is peculiarly beautiful. The sun always descends slowly and regularly until half its disc is concealed, and then it seems instantly to drop out of sight, as if to conceal its blushes over this exposure of his couch.

During the summer evenings, when storms gather about the mountains, the sunsets are most beautiful. The writer has seen several of these; one he remembers most vividly. While he stood gazing at the contending elements the black cloud which veiled the sun suddenly parted, revealing beyond a vista of cloudy embankments a gloriously illuminated chamber of purple and gold, which gradually expanded, changing its tints, until the whole became a heavenly landscape, through which, we fancied, could be seen flowing the pellucid water of the

River of Life. And while we stood entranced, oblivious to surroundings, there descended a gauzy veil, leaving in front of it an avenue of crystal and azure, bounded by walls of gold and sapphire. The next moment there drooped upon these walls banners of scarlet and purple. They remained but a minute, when all vanished. The sun had gone entirely out of sight.

Ascending to the railway station you again enter the coach and are whirled back to the Point along the terrace cut out of the bosom of the mountain, sheer precipices frowning above you, deep gorges yawning beneath you. The ride is short but thrilling, and the impressions you receive will never be effaced.

The train halts at the hotel, which stands upon solid rock, each story having a broad gallery, from which the guests feast their eyes on the beauties above, below and around them. During all seasons of the year the views from this particular spot are charming.

THE INCLINE RAILWAY.

You are now at the head of the Incline, and its pretty car awaits you. The seats are parallel to the rails, but are raised in parquet style, so that passengers may see over each others heads. The faces of the passengers are toward the east, whether ascending or descending. Two great ropes of steel sweep along

"ROCK CITY."

the sheaves between the rails, one drawing your car downward, the other drawing a corresponding car upward. While you gaze a sensation akin to floating in air seizes upon you, and you feel exhilarated. The pleasure continues even when you reach precipitous "Jacob's Ladder," for you are certain of the safety of the machinery. You pass the ascending car, and salute its occupants, and once more look out over the beautiful valley. Soon you see the breath of white steam arising from the building at the foot of the Incline, in the tower of which you discover the engineer who guides your car. The engines and hoisting machinery are beneath his feet.

From the Incline station you can return by horse car to the city, passing in full view of the South Tredegar Iron Works, the Abbattoir, Tannery, Blast Furnace, the handsome residences on College Hill and East Terrace, the Palace Hotel and Read House, and alight at the Union Passenger Depot.

3. BY THE INCLINE AND NARROW GAUGE.

You take horse cars that pass in front of the Union Passenger Depot. These will deliver you, in summer time, at the station of the Lookout Incline. Taking the cosy little car the ascent is made with your face looking down the track, the floor of the car being parallel to the rails. As you ascend you catch glimpses of St. Elmo, of the hills topped with cottages above East Lake, and then of Chattanooga and the Tennessee. In a few minutes you are on the lower gallery of the company's large hotel.

From these galleries you have an exquisite view of the valley and of the cottages and gardens of the field of the

"BATTLE ABOVE THE CLOUDS."

It would seem a pity to spoil the poetic battle which war correspondents created out of the skirmish that occurred on this open space, with its fringe of woods concealing the tall precipice that overhangs the Nashville, Chattanooga & St. Louis Railway, as it skirts the river on its outward passage to the valley on your left. The story related by Gen. Hooker in his report (Conduct of the War, p. 167) would be amusing to you now as you gaze upon this peaceful spot. Hooker says:

"After two or three short but sharp conflicts the plateau was cleared, the enemy, with his reinforcements, driven from the walls and pits around Craven's house, the last point at which he could make a stand in force, and, all broken and dismayed, were hurled over the rocks and precipices into the valley."

What became of those "rocks and precipices" over which Fighting Joe hurled those ill-fated Confederates is a question that not even the "Bohemian" is able to answer. The facts seem to be about as follows:

On November 23, 1863, Gen. Hooker's corps encamped in the valley west of where you stand. A battery of rifled guns was planted on Moccasin Bend, in front. The Federal army occupied the city of Chattanooga. The Confederates were in possession of Lookout Mountain top, and occupied the pallisades and the plateau beneath you, the valley on the east and Missionary Ridge.

About 11 o'clock of the morning of the 24th the battery on Moccasin Bend opened furiously on the Confederates in the valley, while Hooker advanced from the west. Skirmishing soon began on the western side of the mountain, while a cloud slowly settled down upon the Confedrates, on the plateau, entirely concealing them from the Federals. The Federals were not discovered by the Confederate brigade at Craven's house until they were only a few yards away. For about half an hour the Confederate general—Walthal—kept up a sort of running fire, slowly falling back until fully one-half of his men were made prisoners. Very few were killed on either side, owing to darkness, the movements occurring *in* the cloud and not *above* it. The firing of artillery on the Moccasin and from Fort Negly, near Chattanooga, gave Gen. Hooker his idea of the "roar of battle," and yet Gen. Grant correctly states it when he says "there was no battle fought on Lookout Mountain." During the night firing was kept up, at short intervals, as the Confederates evacuated the mountain, along what is now called the "old road," seen on your right; and when the morning dawned the flag of the Union floated from the Point, having been planted there by a member of the 8th Kentucky Regiment just at dawn. In addition to the heavy fog which covered the valley during the entire night, there was an eclipse of the moon.

Taking the Narrow Gauge coach you are carried along the bosom of the mountain, where, from the valley beneath, the train resembles a tin toy of

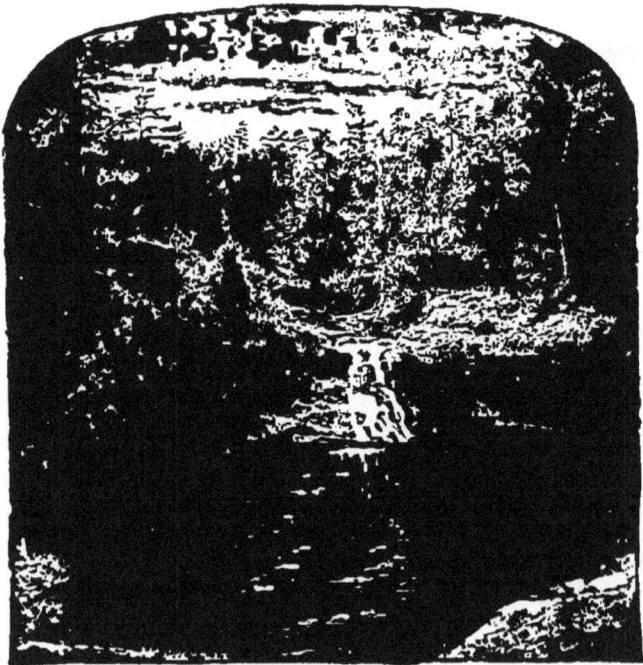

LULU LAKE.

Christmas days, and presently you reach Sunset Rock, which is described in Route 2.

From Sunset Rock you can take carriage for "Natural Bridge" and for Rock City and Lulu Lake, returning to the city by the Broad Gauge Railway, if you prefer.

This is but a hasty examination of Historic Lookout, and is prepared for tourists, who are always in a hurry. Those who have leisure can spend weeks upon its lofty summit, enjoying its breezes in summer time, and its dry air in winter. They can dream of the Indian possession; yes, of the Indians who came and disappeared before the Cherokees, and can read the story of the Cherokee possession and ejectment. And then they can visit the camping grounds of the armies of the Union and of the Confederacy; the site of the great hospital, and of the corn mill that stood at the head of the glen, when the Western Republic was passing under the tribulum of disintegration. Though the writer wore the grey, and has ever been true to the sunny land of his adoption, he never visits this mountain without thanking God that there is but one Country, one Union, one Constitution; and offering a silent prayer that He will continue in the future, as He has done in the past, to take care of His own.

JOHN ROSS HOUSE.

THE BATTLE-FIELDS.

The three battles of the war for the preservation of the Union which have made this section famous are—in the order of their occurrence—the Battle of Lookout Mountain, the Battle of Chickamauga, and the Battle of Missionary Ridge. Of these we will attempt general outlines only.

Lookout is reached by railways described elsewhere. Missionary Ridge is reached by the Electric Railway and by the Chattanooga, Rome & Columbus Railway. Chickamauga is reached by carriage over the Rossville turnpike, and by the trains of the Chattanooga, Rome & Columbus Railway.

If you desire to visit Chickamauga by carriage from Chattanooga you will drive out through Chattanooga Valley, over the Rossville turnpike road, and, passing the John Ross House, turn to the left. When you reach the corner of the Kelley farm you will enter the battle-field of Saturday, and if your guide is posted, you will be shown where brilliant charges and scenes of carnage laid many a noble spirit low. Even at this late day much attention is given to ou ting down trees scarred with bullet-holes. Every bullet has left its cicatrix, and many a tree shows a score of wounds.

Soon you emerge upon a glade, on the southern skirts of which the Federals threw up the temporary breast-works on the night of the 19th. Crossing the Lafayette highway again, you take a country road and drive to the residence of G. W. Snodgrass—himself a landmark of the early days of Chattanooga—which stands at the base of Horseshoe Ridge, on which General Thomas established his headquarters, and where the fiercest struggle of that terrible two days' battle occurred on the evening of Sunday, September 20th. This humble cabin was then used as a hospital, and as you now stand in the shadow of its surrounding shade trees you can look up to the beautiful knoll, sleeping in peace, and dream of that terrible day when brother fell by the hand of brother in a most unnecessary and ever-to-be-regretted war.

From the Snodgrass House the visitor can travel by neighborhood and public roads to the well known points of the field; from McAfee's Church to Crawfish Springs. The tour can easily be made in one day.

If you prefer to visit Chickamauga by railway, take the train in the Central Passenger Depot. The first stop will be on the summit of Missionary Ridge. The next will be "Chickamauga Battle-field" Station. There you will leave your train, unless you prefer to continue on to Crawfish Springs.

Close to this station is the site of Widow Glenn's House. There remain only the decayed gate-posts, the stone-walled well, the scattered bricks of the chimney, and a couple of peach trees. At this writing these are discovered in a

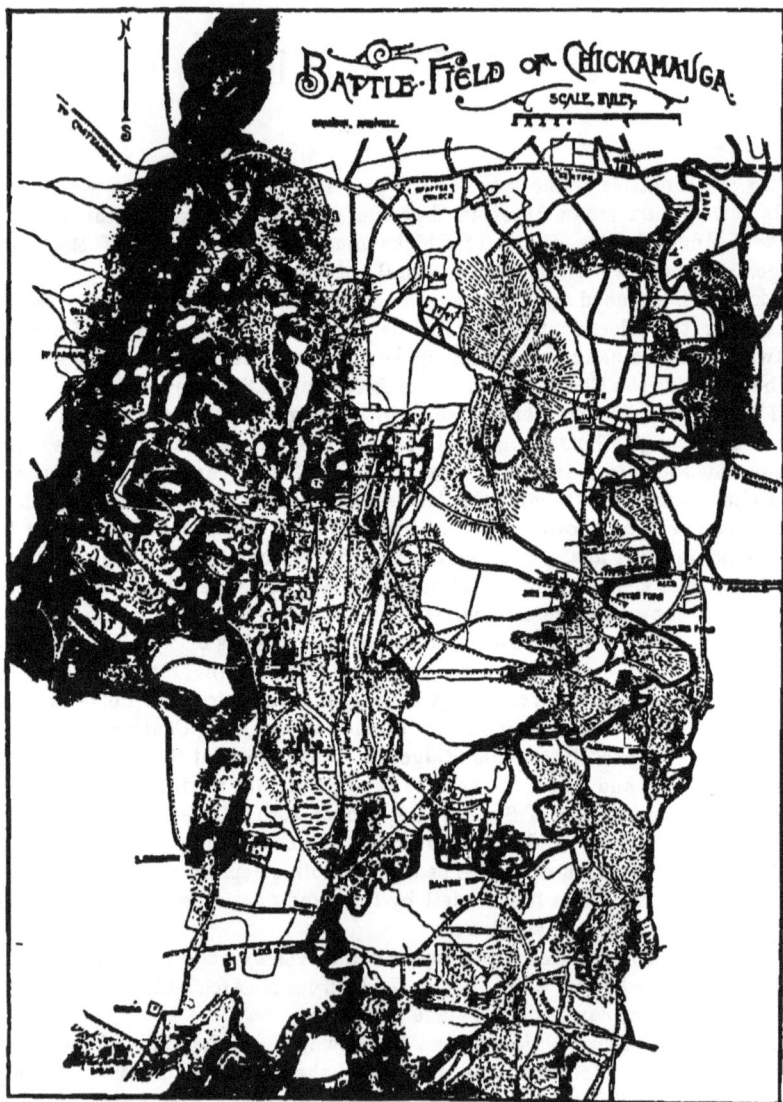

BATTLE-FIELD OF CHICKAMAUGA

corner of a growing field of wheat. A few hundred yards distant the gallant Lytle fell, when Longstreet made his brilliant charge.

It is about one and a half miles from this station to the Snodgrass House and Horseshoe Ridge; a half mile east of that ridge is the Kelley House, on the farm that "formed the key of the Union position."

No tourist should fail to visit Crawfish Springs, not only because there began the sanguinary battle, but because of the natural wonder. A livery stable at that point will accommodate all visitors desiring to drive over the field.

The several points of historic interest in the Battle of Missionary Ridge can be reached by the Union Railway, the Electric Railway and the O., R. & C. Railway. Orchard Knob is a station on the Union Railway, and Sherman Heights on the E. T., V. & G. Railway. In fact, all the battle-fields can be easily and comfortably visited.

BATTLE OF CHICKAMAUGA.

On the 8th of September, 1863, General Bragg, of the Confederate army, having discovered that the Federal army threatened his left and rear, evacuated Chattanooga, and it was immediately occupied by General Rosecrans, of the Federal army, thus winning the prize of the campaign without firing a gun. The pursuit of the Confederates was soon undertaken, and when this movement began Bragg attempted to flank Rosecrans and throw his army between the main Federal army and the garrison at Chattanooga. On the 18th of September both armies stood glaring at each other on the banks of the Chickamauga— murky "River of Death." Bragg had received reinforcements from the Army of Virginia, under Longstreet.

On the 18th there was considerable skirmishing and manœuvering for position, and on the 19th the storm burst with pitiless fury. By 10 A. M. the engagement was general; now the Confederates were routed, only to rally and hurl back, with sickening slaughter, the hosts of the Union. Until late in the afternoon the conflict raged, when suddenly an ominous lull fell upon the dead, the dying and the weary. Not a gun was heard for over an hour. Rosecrans was deceived into the belief that his enemy had been sufficiently punished for one day, and began the execution of strategic movements; but scarcely had the hour ended when a furious charge by the Confederates threw the Federal lines into confusion, and had it not been for the twenty guns of Hazen, on the Rossville road, the day would have closed with a most telling victory for the Confederates. The galling enfilading fire of this artillery compelled the Confederates to fall back as the sun went down beyond distant Lookout.

When darkness enveloped the bloody scene, arrangements were made for burying the dead and caring for the wounded by both sides. Bragg reformed his lines soon after nightfall, and placed them in direct command of Polk, on the right, with five divisions, and Longstreet, on the left, with six divisions. This changing of organization in the face of the enemy proved to be a fatal mistake. The quaint reply of Mr. Lincoln when asked to commit a similar blunder should have been repeated to the Confederate General: "It is a bad plan to swap

4

horses in the middle of a stream." Bragg might not have heeded the homely wisdom, for the fates had already written failure over against his name.

Polk was ordered to strike at dawn of the 20th, but the reverend general slept away from his lines during the night of the 19th, and used the early daylight of the 20th to read a newspaper at Alexander's bridge, which, as Bragg angrily told General D. H. Hill, "was two miles from the line of battle, where he ought to have been fighting." Polk did not begin the executing of Bragg's order until nearly 9 o'clock, a delay which cost him his command. When he began the assault, the entire line was quickly involved. Back went the Confederate right, but almost instantly rallied. Charge after charge attested. the heroism of the combatants. The onslaught on the Federal left ceased when the irresistible charges of the Confederates broke their center. Then, it is said, Rosecrans made several fatal mistakes. Certain it is that he telegraphed to Washington his army was defeated. Great soldier though he was, he had lost his head.

Thomas maintained his ground and gallantly withstood the charges of the Confederates, now flushed with victory. "Like a lion at bay he repulsed the terrible onslaughts of the enemy" on the knoll above the Snodgrass House, where he had ordered the artillery massed to make his last stand. Strong lines of infantry, commanded by Brannan and Steedman, skirted this elevated spot, which resisted with almost unparalleled gallantry the assaults on their front and flanks. As the sun began to go down behind the tall pines, on that Sabbath afternoon, the storm burst anew around the Snodgrass knoll. Charge after charge was repelled with terrible slaughter to both sides. The dead lay in heaps along the green slopes, and the groans of the wounded rent the air as darkness enveloped the enraged combatants, and Thomas sorrowfully began his retreat to Rossville, leaving the field and most of his dead and wounded in possession of the Confederates.

Gen. Hill makes this allusion to the opposing generals in a foot note to his excellent paper in the Century:

"Bragg had great respect and affection for the first lieutenant of his battery. The tones of tenderness with which he spoke of 'Old Tom' are still well remembered by me.

"Both of these illustrious Southerners dropped dead of heart disease: Thomas in San Francisco in 1870, and Bragg in Galveston in 1876. Did the strain upon them in those terrible days at Chickamauga hasten their death?"

On the following day Thomas placed his lines around Chattanooga, while Bragg, instead of pursuing his victory, took possession of Missionary Ridge, Chattanooga Valley and the summit of Lookout. His hope was to starve the army now blockaded in Chattanooga. To accomplish this he seized the railway at the point of Lookout Mountain.

The Confederate Gen. Hill bears testimony to the courage of his great opponent in these words:

"Thomas had received orders after Granger's arrival to retreat to Rossville, but, stout soldier as he was, he resolved to hold his ground until nightfall. An hour more of daylight would have insured his capture. Thomas had under him all the Federal army, except the six brigades which had been driven off by the left wing."

Gen. Fullerton tells the story of one of the terrible charges on the Horseshoe in these few words:

"The enemy massed a force to retake the ridge. They came before our men had rested; twice they assaulted and were driven back. During one assault, as the first line came within range of our muskets, it halted, apparently hesitating, when we saw a colonel seize a flag, wave it over his head, and rush forward. The whole line instantly caught his enthusiasm, and with a wild cheer followed, only to be hurled back again. Our men ran down the ridge in pursuit. In the midst of a group of Confederate dead and wounded they found the brave colonel dead, the flag he carried spread over him where he fell."

A month after the disaster of Chickamauga Gen. Rosecrans was relieved and Gen. Thomas was placed in command of the Army of the Cumberland.

Rosecrans and Bragg have been censured for their conduct of this battle. Strange to say, neither general took advantage of the mistakes of the other. It is beyond controversy that the Federal general was the abler commander of the two. It is pretty generally conceded that had Bragg been Rosecran's equal the gallant Army of the Cumberland would have been annihilated. Bragg repeated the tactics of Cave City, Perryville and Murfreesboro, and again allowed victory to escape.

Rosecrans' order to Wood to "close upon Reynolds and support him," and his hasty return to Chattanooga from the field, are said to have been fatal blunders. The Confederate Gen. Hill says this of the first mistake:

"Brannan was between Reynolds and Wood. The order 'to close upon Reynolds' was naturally enough interpreted by Wood to support Reynolds, and not, as it seems Rosecrans meant, to close to the left. He withdrew his division and began his march to the left and in rear of Brannan. A gap was left into which Longstreet stepped with the eight brigades (Bushrod Johnson's, McNair's, Gregg's, Kershaw's, Law's, Humphreys', Benning's and Robertson's), which he had arranged in three lines to constitute his grand column of attack. Davis' two brigades, one of Van Cleve's, and Sheridan's entire division were caught in front and flank and driven from the field. Disregarding the order of the day, Longstreet now gave the order to wheel to the right instead of the left, and thus take in reverse the strong position of the enemy. Five of McCook's brigades were speedily driven off the field. He estimates their loss at forty per cent."

The part played by Longstreet in this battle was worthy of his great fame in those days. The rapid transfer of his troops from Virginia to Georgia was kept a profound secret from the Federals. On the 15th of September Gen. Halleck telegraphed to Gen. Rosecrans that Bragg had not been re-enforced from Virginia. At that moment Bragg and Longstreet may have been shaking hands. Indeed, Longstreet's arrival was as great a surprise to Rosecrans as was Napoleon's descent upon Marengo to Gen. Melas. He seemed to have dropped out of the heavens. This should go to Gen. Rosencrans' credit.

Gen. Hill relates an incident of the battle, which is full of pathos, and worthy of perpetuity. The general tells: "In the lull of the strife I went with a staff officer to examine the ground on our left. One of Helm's wounded men had been overlooked, and was lying alone in the woods, his head partly supported by a tree. He was shockingly injured. He belonged to Von Zinken's regiment, of New Orleans, composed of French, Germans and Irish. I said to him: 'My poor fellow, you are badly hurt. What regiment do you belong to?' He replied: 'The Fifth Confederit, and a dommed good regiment it is.' The answer, though almost ludicrous, touched me as illustrating the *esprit de corps* of the soldier—his pride in and his affection for his command. Col. Von Zinken told me afterward that one of his desperately wounded Irishmen cried out to his comrades: 'Charge them, boys; they have cha-ase (cheese) in their haversacks.' Poor Pat, he has fought courageously in every land in quarrels not his own."

And on the same field where lay this son of Erin fell the gallant Gen. W. H. Lytle, who wrote

"I am dying, Egypt, dying,
Ebbs the crimson life-tide fast."

Col. Archer Anderson estimates the relative strength of the two armies: "From an examination of the original returns in the War Department, I reckon, in round numbers, the Federal infantry and artillery on the field at fifty-nine thousand, and the Confederate infantry and artillery at fifty-five thousand. The Federal cavalry, about ten thousand strong, was outnumbered by the Confederates by a thousand men. Thus speak the returns. Perhaps a deduction of five thousand men from the reported strength of each army would more nearly represent the actual strength of the combatants. It is, I think, certain that Rosecrans was stronger in infantry and artillery than Bragg by at least four thousand men."

Of these fully twenty-seven thousand were killed or wounded.

We make the following extract from the small war volume issued by Gen. H. M. Cist, entitled "The Army of the Cumberland." Gen. Cist was A. A. G. on the staff of Gen. Rosecrans, and afterward on the staff of Gen. Thomas:

"All things considered, the battle of Chickamauga, for the forces engaged, was the hardest fought and bloodiest battle of the Rebellion. . . . .

"To the enemy, the results of the engagement proved a victory barren of any lasting benefits, and produced no adequate results to the immense drain on the resources of his army. In a number of places Bragg's official report shows that his army was so crippled that he was not able to strengthen one portion of his line, when needed, with troops from another part of the field; and after the conflict was over, his army was so cut up that it was impossible for him to follow up his apparent success and secure possession of the objective point of the campaign—Chattanooga. This great gateway of the mountains remaining in possession of the Army of the Cumberland, after Bragg had paid the heavy price he did at Chickamauga, proves that his battle was a victory only in name, and a careful examination of the results and their cost will show how exceedingly small it was to the enemy."

So much is all that our space permits for the story of the sanguinary field of Chickamauga. No wonder the blue and the grey are now united in an effort to erect thereon memorials of American valor, as has already been done at Gettysburg. No wonder that Wheeler, one of the great cavalry generals on the Confederate side, and now a member of Congress, hurries to meet Rosecrans in this year of national peace and prosperity, 1889, to help establish the battle lines and positions, and lay out the boundaries of a park that shall be a Mecca to those who honor the memory of Rosecrans, Bragg, Thomas, Longstreet, Granger, Hill, Brannan, Breckinridge, Steedman, Cleburne, Wheeler, Lytle, and the rest of the heroes who participated in the conflict. And the inquiry then will not be, "Who won the battle?" but "Who fought the Bravest and died the Purest?" on both sides. In deed and in truth it will then be acknowledged a "drawn battle."

BATTLE OF MISSIONARY RIDGE.

The Federal authorities allude to this series of combats as the "Battles of Chattanooga, Lookout Mountain and Missionary Ridge."

On the 18th of October, 1863, Gen. U. S. Grant assumed command of the Department of Tennessee and Gen. George H. Thomas remained in command of the Army of the Cumberland. The Confederates held Lookout Mountain and the railway at its base, as well as the valley of Chattanooga and Missionary Ridge.

The Federal base of supplies was at Bridgeport and Stevenson, fifty-one miles distant by wagon road, and they were transported by wagons through Sequachee Valley, and over the mountains that surround Chattanooga. As the autumn advanced this mountain road became almost impassable, and starvation threatened the garrison of the mountain city. By a well planned and skillfully executed strategic movement Lookout Valley was opened on October 28th, and on November 1st the "siege of Chattanooga, by the forces of nature," was raised. The Confederates were still on the Federal front, on Lookout and Missionary Ridge, and in the Chattanooga Valley.

We learn from official reports that on the 15th of November, 1863, Gen. Grant had concentrated 80,000 troops in and around Chattanooga, and that 50,000 Confederates occupied Lookout and Missionary Ridge, Longstreet having gone on a "wild goose chase" to Knoxville. On the 23d, Grant undertook the raising of the seige on his front by ordering Gen. Thomas to make an armed reconnaissance to develop the Confederate lines, which was done in the early morning By 1 P. M. Sherman had crossed the Tennessee at the northern extremity of Missionary Ridge, and at 4 o'clock he had a heavy engagement in an effort to seize the second hill of the Ridge, the one through which passes the railway tunnel. He was repulsed ; Granger had already captured "Orchard Knob," and soon darkness closed the combat.

If the reader will drive out to the site of Fort Wood he will at a glance take in the positions of both armies on that day. Where you stand, great guns frowned defiance to the enemy entrenched on Missionary Ridge in front. Between you and the Ridge is the conical mound, with its houses and scrubby shade, known as Orchard Knob, and held a part of that day by the Confederates. Beyond this knob is Missionary Ridge, now covered with orchards and vineyards, and dotted with happy homes, but on that day of strife rocky and wrinkled with ravines, and uninhabited. The northern extremity of this ridge is where Sherman ascended, and the second and lowest depression south of it is where the railroad sweeps through a tunnel.

Early in the morning of the 24th the movements were continued. Hooker bridged swollen Lookout Creek, in full view of Stevenson, whose lines were posted on the summit of Lookout. The mist hanging over the valley concealed from the observatory of the Confederates the advancing column of the Federal Geary. The Confederate Gen. Walthal, with a small force, held the terrace of the mountain, just under the "Point," known as the Craven place, over which Hooker would have to pass to reach the valley of Chattanooga. The skirmishing on that lofty field we briefly describe elsewhere as the "Battle Above the Clouds."

On the 25th began the battle of Missionary Ridge proper. During the long, long day the battle raged with relentless fury. At 4 P. M. the Federal lines, which filled the valley, moved rapidly forward, at a signal of six guns, fired in rapid succession on Orchard Knob, up the slopes of the rifle-pits of the Confederates, under a galling and destructive fire of musketry. Over the rifle-pits, thinly occupied by the depleted division of the Confederates, but gallantly defended, swept line after line of the victorious Federals, and when the sun went down the Confederates were routed, the Federals held the Ridge, and from that time forward remained in undisputed possession of Chattanooga.

The battle was fierce and decisive, and the losses very heavy. Bragg said in his report: "The enemy having secured much of our artillery, soon availed themselves of our panic, and, turning our guns upon us, enfiladed our lines both right and left, rendering them wholly untenable." Grant said "they encountered a fearful volley of grape and cannister from near thirty pieces of artillery and musketry from still well-filled rifle-pits on the summit." Both sides recognized this battle as one of the most important and decisive of the war, and one in which both armies displayed the highest courage and the most brilliant feats of gallantry.

The Confederates retreated in the direction of Ringgold, by way of Chickamauga Station, leaving behind 600 prisoners and a host of stragglers, forty cannon and 7,000 stand of small arms.

Next morning Sherman pushed on to Graysville, and Palmer and Hooker took the Rossville road. At Ringgold the Confederates, under the brilliant Cleburne, turned and attacked Hooker. It was a severe combat, lasting the entire day. The Federals suffered large losses, many being experienced officers. Bragg continued on to Dalton, and Grant sent relief to Burnside, who was closely invested at Knoxville by Longstreet. That was the first result of Missionary Ridge.

The following extract from Gen. Cist's book may add a little spice to our tame description of this battle, and is inserted without comment:

"On the crest of the hill Bragg's men had constructed their heaviest breast-works, protected on our front by some fifty pieces of artillery in position. As our troops advanced, each command cheering and answering back the cheers of the others, the men broke into a double-quick, all striving to be the first to reach the rifle-pits at the foot of the ridge, held by a strong line of the enemy's troops. The Confederates opened fire with shot and shell from their batteries as our troops advanced, changing it soon to grape and cannister, which, with the fire from the infantry, made it terrifically hot. Dashing through this, over an open plain, our soldiers swept on, driving the enemy's skirmishers, charging down on the line of works at the foot of the ridge, capturing it at the point of the bayonet, and routing the rebels, sending them at full speed up the ridge, killing and capturing them in great numbers. The troops lay down at the foot of the ridge awaiting orders. Under no orders from their officers, first one regiment and then another started with its colors up the ascent, until, with loud hurrahs, the entire line, cheered by their officers, advanced over and around rocks, under and through the fallen timber, charged up the ridge, each determined to reach the summit first. In some cases the Confederates were bayoneted at their guns. The charge occupied about one hour from the time of the firing of the guns on Orchard Knob until our troops occupied the rebel lines on the ridge."

* * * * * * * * * * * . * * *

Sherman says: "Grant told me 'that the men of Thomas' army had been so demoralized by the battle of Chickamauga that he feared they could not be got out of their trenches to assume the offensive,' and that 'the Army of the Cumberland had so long been in the trenches that he wanted my troops to hurry up to take the offensive *first*, after which he had no doubt the Cumberland Army would fight well.' So, under Grant's plan, the Army of the Cumberland was to stand by and be taught a grand object lesson how to fight, as given by Sherman.

* * * * * * * * * * * * * *

"Whenever the victory of Missionary Ridge shall be narrated on history's page, the gallant charge of the brave men of Wood's and Sheridan's divisions, with those of Baird and Johnson on the left and right, will always be the prominent feature of the engagement as told in the coming years, and will be the last to lose its glory and renown.

"No wonder that Gen. Grant failed to appreciate this movement at the time, not understanding the troops who had it in charge. When he found these commands ascending the ridge to capture it when he ordered a 'demonstration' to be made to the foot of the hill and there to wait, he turned sharply to Gen. Thomas and asked, 'By whose orders are those troops going up the hill?' Gen. Thomas, taking in the situation at once, suggested that it was probably by their own. Gen. Grant remarked that 'it was all right if it turned out all right,' and added, 'if not, some one will suffer.' But it turned out 'all right,' and Grant in his official report compliments the troops for 'following closely the retreating enemy without further orders.'"

Gen. Grant thus describes the ascent of Missionary Ridge: "The troops moved forward, drove the enemy from the rifle-pits at the base of the ridge like bees from a hive, stopped but a moment until the whole were in line, and commenced the ascent of the mountain from right to left almost simultaneously, following closely the retreating foe without further orders. They encountered a fearful volley of grape and cannister from near thirty pieces of artillery and musketry from still well-filled rifle-pits on the summit, but not a waver was seen in all that long line of brave men. The progress was steadily onward, until the summit was in their possession."

Gen. Bragg gives the Confederate story thus:

"About half-past 3 P. M. the immense force in front of our left and center advanced in three lines, preceded by heavy skirmishers. Our batteries opened with fine effect, and much confusion was produced before they reached musket range. In a short time the roar of musketry became very heavy, and it was soon apparent that the enemy was repulsed in my immediate front. While riding along the crest congratulating the troops, intelligence reached me that our line was broken on my right and the enemy had crowned the ridge."

The Confederate Gen. D. H. Hill, commenting on those days, says: "There was no more splendid fighting in '61, when the flower of the Southern youth was in the field, than was displayed in the bloody days of September, '63. But it seems to me that the *élan* of the Southern soldier was never seen after Chickamauga—that brilliant dash which had distinguished him on a hundred fields was gone forever. He was too intelligent not to know that the cutting in two of Georgia meant death to all his hopes. He knew that Longstreet's absence was imperiling Lee's safety, and that what had to be done must be done quickly. The delay to strike was exasperating to him; the failure to strike after the success was crushing to all his longings for an independent South. He fought stoutly to the last, but, after Chickamauga, with the sullenness of despair and without the enthusiasm of hope. That 'barren victory' sealed the fate of the Southern Confederacy."

A war correspondent, whose letters have been remodeled into a book, says of this battle, in the peculiar style of his class:

"The splendid march from the Federal line of battle to the crest was made in one hour and five minutes, but it was a grander march toward the end of carnage—a glorious campaign of sixty-five minutes toward the white borders of peace. It made that fleeting November afternoon imperishable."

The Confederates were more seriously affected by the disaster of Missionary Ridge than had been the Federals by the defeat of Chickamauga. The depleted ranks of the Confederates could not be replenished, for there were no men left in the rear to draw from. The whole world was open to the recruiting persuasions of the United States Government.

We do not doubt that the Almighty permitted the Confederacy to work out its defeat in the West through the incompetency of Gen. Bragg. At Perryville he lost the confidence of Hardee and Polk. Confidence was still lacking in wing, corps and division commanders at Murfreesboro. Chickamauga added to the general discontent, and then Missionary Ridge made forbearance a crime. Joseph E. Johnston came too late, but the retreat upon Atlanta has placed the name of Johnston next to that of Lee. Every true American soldier is proud of the valor of Thomas, Grant, Lee and Johnston, and in their exalted moments forget to boast of which side they belonged to, and sincerely rejoice that they are now citizens of a country that produced such men.

CHICKAMAUGA NATIONAL PARK.

On the 28th and 30th of April, 1889, Col. Kellogg, U. S. A., accompanied by Gens. Rosecrans, Reynolds, Wheeler, and other participants in the great battle of Chickamauga, visited the field to make accurate locations of troops, with a view to the establishment of a National Park. The veterans of both armies are deeply interested in this movement.

Not only is it desirable that this Park should be established as an eternal memorial to American valor, and that tablets should be erected to commemorate special exhibitions of that valor, but the Government should establish there a Soldiers' Home, modeled after the one so successfully conducted at Dayton, Ohio. And into that Home might be admitted the disabled citizens who served in both armies. We say "might," because we know that such unselfish patriotism is impossible, inasmuch as the politicians, not the brave men who fought the battle on the Union side, would oppose such generosity.

The writer religiously believes that if the matter was submitted to the vote of the Union soldiers—skulkers, bummers and camp followers excluded—the brave men who always bared their breasts to storm of Confederate hail, would unanimously vote to admit the disabled of their gallant enemy to the comforts and blessings of such a paradise. Aye, more! They would vote the gathering of the ashes of their brave opponents who fell at Chickamauga, Chattanooga and Missionary Ridge, into the beautiful National Cemetery. But the brave veterans of the Union will never have the opportunity to so vote.

SOME DISTANCES.

The following table will be of interest to those who desire to study the movements of troops during the battles of Chattanooga, Chickamauga and Missionary Ridge:

FROM CHATTANOOGA TO

Orchard Knob	2 miles.	National Cemetery	1½ miles.
Sherman Heights	5 "	Boyce Station (old)	6 "
Rossville Gap	5 "	McFarland's Gap	7 "
Crawfish Spring	13 "	Lee & Gordon Mill	12 "
Widow Glenn's House	10 "	Snodgrass House	9¼ "
Kelley's Ferry	12 "	Ringgold	16 "
La Fayette	24½ "	Wauhatchee	6 "
Lookout Mountain (base)	2¼ "	Brown's Ferry	5 "

FROM ROSSVILLE TO

Horseshoe Ridge	4 miles.	McAfee's Church	3 miles.
Kelley's House	4½ "	Ringgold (via bridge)	12 "

FROM MCFARLAND'S GAP TO

Widow Glenn's House	4	miles.	Lee & Gordon Mill	5¾	miles.
Kelley's House	2¾	"	Crawfish Spring	7¾	"
Snodgrass House	2½	"	Vidito's House	1½	"

FROM WIDOW GLENN'S HOUSE TO

McFarland's Gap	4	miles.	Snodgrass House	1¾	miles.
Lee & Gordon Mill	1¾	"	Vidito's House	1	"
Crawfish Spring	3¾	"	Leet's Tan-yard	½	"
Chattanooga	10	"	Brotherton House	¾	"

CHATTANOOGA AS A MANUFACTURING POINT.

It is now generally conceded that the "Chattanooga mineral district" is one of the richest in coal, iron and copper of this entire continent. The coal is very nearly free from sulphur, and cokes well; the beds of iron ore are abundant, averaging from four to five feet in thickness, and the ores average fifty per cent of iron. The coal is adapted to the manufacture of the best quality of iron, and lies on the great layer of conglomerate rock of the lower carboniferous period, averaging five feet in thickness. The iron ore embraces brown hematite, or limonite, and fossiliferous red hematite, the latter crossed by great beds of limestone of the subcarboniferous period.

For timber, the district draws on a forest that is tributary to Chattanooga by reason of 800 miles of railroad, and more than 1,000 miles of navigable waters, which penetrate it in every direction almost. There is every variety of wood indigenous to the climate of thirty-five degrees north latitude, and a few other varieties considered peculiar to the climate 1,000 miles north of us. There is an abundance of Norway pine, hemlock, black walnut, maple and wild cherry. There is also an abundant supply of yellow pine, together with white and yellow poplar, and perhaps the supply of oak is the largest of all. The hills are plentifully supplied with hickory, and not very far away is red cedar, and on all the ridges mountain laurel grows prolifically. There is also a reasonably good supply of buckeye and wild cucumber.

For the movement of raw material and the distribution of manufactures, Chattanooga's means of transportation are unsurpassed. This coming autumn the great water-way, the Tennessee River, will be relieved from the muscle shoals obstruction, thus opening to us water communication with all the ports of the world. At present there are seven railways, whose termini are in this city—the Western & Atlantic; the Nashville, Chattanooga & St. Louis; the East Tennessee, Virginia & Georgia; the Memphis & Charleston; the Cincinnati Southern; the Alabama Great Southern, and the Chattanooga, Rome & Columbus. If we read the signs correctly, two more trunk lines will be added before the close of 1890.

In demonstration of Chattanooga's importance as a manufacturing point, we quote the larger

MANUFACTORIES

in operation on June 1, 1889, companies and firms:

BLAST FURNACES.

Citico Furnace Company.   Chattanooga Iron Company.

ROLLING MILLS.

Lookout Iron Company.   South Tredegar Iron Company.

Roane Iron Company (temporarily suspended).

TANNERIES.

Fayerweather & Ladew.   Scholze Bro.'s Tannery.

FOUNDRIES.

Etna Foundry (G. W. Wheeland).   Wagner's Foundry.
Cahill's Foundry and Iron Works.   Chattanooga Car Foundry Company.
Chattanooga Pipe and Foundry Co.   Phœnix Foundry Company.

MACHINE SHOPS.

Traxall & Dunnemeyer.   Etna Machine Works.
Cahill Architectural Works.   Meehan Brake Shoe Works.

Chattanooga Machinery Company.

PLANING MILLS.

Loomis & Hart Manufacturing Co.   Willingham Lumber Company.
Duncan, Pytt & Company.   Seymour, Stratton & Company.
Lookout Planing Mill.   East Tennessee Manufacturing Co.
Morrison Manufacturing Company.   Hughes Lumber Company.

STOVE FACTORIES.

Chattanooga Stove Company.   Snow Stove and Range Company.

Gibson-Love Manufacturing Company.

IRON AND VITRIFIED PIPES.

Chattanooga Iron Pipe Works.   Montague's Clay Pipe Works.

Chattanooga Clay Pipe Works.

FURNITURE.

Loomis & Hart Manufacturing Co.   Temple & Shipp Furniture Company.
Sundquist Manufacturing Company.   Ristine & Co. Furniture Company.

WAGON FACTORIES.

Fassnacht's Carriage and Wagon Factory.

AGRICULTURAL IMPLEMENTS.

Chattanooga Tool Works.   Chattanooga Plow Works.

Chattanooga Agricultural Works.

MISCELLANEOUS.

Chattanooga Boiler Works.   Cracker and Candy Factory.
Fruit Canning Company.   Big Spring Ice Company.
Lookout Ice Factory and Storage.   Lowe's Mineral Paint Mill.
Chattanooga Medicine Company.   Standard Scales Works.
Vehicle Springs Company.   Four Cigar Factories.
Palmer's Artificial Stone Works.   Chattanooga Marble and Stone Company.
Troutt's Marble and Granite Yard.   Stewart Electrical (Talc) Appliances.

As the supply of coal, iron and timber is practically inexhaustible, it is confidently predicted that Chattanooga will be one of the largest manufacturing cities of the country before the close of the century.

The manufacturer who has an eye to economy (and what successful manufacturer has not?) must be profoundly impressed with this valley's attractions. Not only is iron, coal and timber cheaper here than in the North, but the actual cost of running a factory is less. Here factories have to be heated not over three months in the year, with occasional demands during another month. At the North this heating period extends to six months, with occasional demands on the seventh. And this item of fuel enters into the calculations of the artizan and laborer, and into the personal expenses of the managers. There is a net saving of fifty per centum.

The saving extends further to the artizan. The mild climate renders the heavy and expensive clothing of the North unwearable. Here is a large item of saving to the families of the workmen. Provisions are about as cheap as elsewhere. The items of saving arising out of balmy climate not only include fuel and clothing, but doctors' bills and medicines. Only the careless suffer here from the unavoidable sicknesses of the North.

The depleting effects of summer heat, common to the lower South, are not felt among the mountains that stand around Chattanooga. At times the sun comes down with scorching rays at midday, just as it comes down all over the Union, but the warm nights which deprive one of restful slumber do not average six per annum in any decade. This statement is based upon an experience acquired during a residence of eighteen years in this city of Chattanooga. See our article on "Climate."

CITY GOVERNMENT.

The city is divided into eight wards, the boundaries of which are too irregular for description in this Guide.

The government is vested in a Mayor and Board of Aldermen (two from each of the eight wards), Recorder (or Police Judge), Auditor, Attorney, Engineer, Tax Assessor and Treasurer, and a Register of Vital Statistics. The Aldermen are organized into six committees: Finance, Streets and Sewers, Fire, Water and Lights, Health and Hospitals, Schools and Public Buildings, and Police and Prisons.

The Board of Health is composed of the Mayor, the Chairman of Health and Hospitals Committee, the City Physician, and a physician chosen by vote of the Board.

The Police are under control of a Police Commission, consisting of two Democrats and one Republican, appointed by the Governor of the State. Each serves for three years, one going out each year.

NOTE—This special organization goes into effect November, 1889. The form at this writing (June 1, 1889) is a Mayor, Board of six Aldermen, Auditor, Attorney, Engineer, Physician, Treasurer and Tax Collector, and a Register of Vital Statistics. The Mayor is now Police Judge.

WATER WORKS.

The Pumping Station is near to the mouth of Citico Creek, and the daily capacity is 20,000,000 gallons. Water is taken at a point 200 feet above Citico Creek, forced through the system of filters (eighteen in number) known as the "National," and sent into town in a twenty-inch main and in a sixteen-inch main. A reservoir is on the side of Missionary Ridge, at Ridgedale, which is 182 feet above Market street, giving a pressure of seventy-five pounds uniformly. The mains are about sixty miles in length. This is just double the length of the mains in the year 1886, and extensions are going on rapidly. There are 200 fire plugs.

FIRE DEPARTMENT.

Headquarters, W. Ninth street, corner of Poplar.

Lookout No. 1, W. Ninth street, corner of Poplar.

Carlisle No. 2, Montgomery avenue, corner of Cowart street.

There are three steam fire-engines, four hose-reels, two hook and ladder trucks, 6,500 feet of hose, and three engine-houses.

FIRE ALARM TELEGRAPH.

The Gamewell system is in use, with the necessary gongs, indicators, and thirty-two alarm boxes, located as follows:

12. Georgia avenue and E. Fourth.	36. Boyce and Hooke.
13. Douglas and Vine.	37. Lookout Engine-house.
14. McCallie avenue and Houston.	41. Gilmer and Palmetto.
15. Walnut and E. Seventh.	42. King and E. Ninth.
16. Gilmer and E.	43. King and E. T. R. R. crossing.
17. Poplar and Fifth.	45. Market and Eighth.
21. Cedar and W. Sixth.	46. Georgia avenue and E. Ninth.
23. Pine and W. Fourth.	51. Market and Union.
24. Market and Second.	52. Whiteside and Aiken.
25. Market and Fourth.	53. John and William.
26. Market and Sixth.	54. Wason Car Works.
27. Loomis & Hart's Mill.	56. Whiteside and Missionary avenue.
31. Gillespie and East Terrace.	57. Hughes' Planing Mill.
32. Roane Iron Company.	62. Carlile Engine-house.
34. Tannery.	121. Read House.
35. College and Cravens.	

Keys can be found at the nearest houses to the boxes, and one is given to each police officer, and a few are given to responsible citizens.

Gongs in engine-houses have indicators attached, and alarm signals will be understood as follows: When an alarm is given from box 36, the bell at the Lookout Engine-house will strike three slowly, and then after a pause it will strike six—thus: 1, 1, 1—1, 1, 1, 1, 1, 1=36. This will be repeated three times, giving four signals for each call of fire.

NEWSPAPERS.

The *Daily* and *Weekly Times*. Published by The Times Printing Company. Office in Adams' Block, Eighth street.

The *Evening News*. Published by Evening News Company.

The *Sunday Argus*. Office on Seventh street.

The *Tradesman*. A monthly devoted to manufactures, and published from the *Times* building.

BANKS.

First National, chartered 1866	capital,	$200,000
Third National, chartered 1881	capital,	250,000
Chattanooga National, chartered 1887	capital,	300,000
City Savings, chartered 1886	capital,	200,000
The Peoples, chartered 1887	capital,	200,000
Trust and Banking Company, chartered 1888	capital,	30,000
Chattanooga Savings, chartered 1889	capital,	50,000
Fourth National, chartered 1889	capital,	150,000

FIRST NATIONAL BANK

SOCIETIES.

MASONIC—Two lodges, one Chapter and a Commandery.
ODD FELLOWS—Two lodges, and an Encampment.
KNIGHTS OF PYTHIAS—Two lodges, Endowment Rank and Uniform Rank.
UNITED WORKMEN—One lodge, second Tuesdays.
ROYAL ARCANUM—One lodge, fourth Mondays.
LEGION OF HONOR—One council, first Mondays.
FRATERNAL LEGION—One camp, first Thursdays.
KNIGHTS OF HONOR—One lodge, first Wednesdays.
CATHOLIC KNIGHTS—Branch No. 71, Sundays.
TURN-VEREIN—Meets every Sunday.
GRAND ARMY OF REPUBLIC—Two posts.
CONFEDERATE VETERANS—One camp.

YOUNG MEN'S CHRISTIAN ASSOCIATION—Rooms in Adams' Block.
CHATTANOOGA MEDICAL SOCIETY—First Fridays.
HEBREW LADIES' BENEVOLENT SOCIETY—Call of president.

BOARD OF TRADE.

Rooms in Chamber of Commerce building, Market street.

CHAMBER OF COMMERCE.

Hall up-stairs, in No. — Market street, rear of building.

PUBLIC LIBRARY.

In same building with the Chamber of Commerce, front room.

ORPHANS' HOME.

On Vine street. Conducted by the ladies of the Woman's Christian Association.

STEELE ORPHANS' HOME.

For colored orphans, on Strait street. Conducted by Mrs. Almira S. Steele, its founder.

ASSOCIATED CHARITIES.

Conducted by a board of trustees and a superintendent. Funds obtained from city and county governments chiefly.

SOME IMPORTANT LAWS.

The following laws are quoted with special reference to Tennessee:

"A homestead in the possession of each head of a family, and the improvements thereon to the extent of $1,000, shall be exempt from sale under legal process during the life of such head of a family; to inure to the benefit of the widow, shall be exempt during the minority of their children occupying the same; nor shall the same be alienated without the joint consent of the husband and wife, when that relation exists. This exemption shall not operate against public taxes, nor debts contracted for the purchase money of such homestead or improvements thereon.

"Married women owning a separate estate, settled upon them and for their separate use, can dispose of the same by will, deed, or otherwise, in as full and complete a manner as if she were unmarried. The property of the wife is not liable for the debts of the husband incurred before marriage. The same law is applicable to the husband. Money deposited in bank by a married woman is free from the claims of husbands or their creditors.

"Under the revenue laws of Tennessee, all property owned in the State, excepting $1,000 worth of personalty belonging to the heads of families, is subject to taxation for State and county purposes. The tax on property levied by the State is forty cents on the $100 worth, ten cents of which shall be for school purposes. Merchants pay ad valorem and privilege taxes, amounting to seventy cents on the $100 worth, ten cents of which is for free schools. Taxes are also levied upon a great number of privileges and upon polls, the poll-tax being applied to school purposes. The county courts are authorized to levy taxes for general county purposes not to exceed the State tax."

Suits can be brought before a justice of the peace up to $500. Six per cent is the legal interest. If "usury" is proven, the entire interest is forfeited.

HISTORIC POINTS.

The stranger, especially if once a soldier, will find the following quite useful:

PLACES TO VISIT.	HOW TO REACH THEM.	WHERE TO GET ON.	FARE.
Battle Above the Clouds	Incline and Broad Gauge R'ys.	Horse Cars and U. P. Depot	0.25
Chickamauga	Chatta., Rome & Col. Railway.	Central Station............	0.25
Confederate Cemetery ..	Hacks and on foot.............	....	*
Crawfish Springs........	Chatta., Rome & Col. Railway.	Central Station	0.35
Cameron Hill	Hacks and on foot	....	*
East Lake	Union Railway...............	Nuby Street Depot.........	0.05
Lookout Mountain......	Broad Gauge Railway	Union Passenger Depot....	0.25
Lookout Mountain	Incline and Nar. Gauge R'ys...	Horse Cars and Union R'y.	0.25
Missionary Ridge	Electric Railway	From Broad Street out.....	0.05
National Cemetery......	Union Railway.................	Nuby Street Depot.........	0 05
Orchard Knob..........	Union Railway.................	Nuby Street Depot........	0.05
Sherman Heights	East Tenn., Va. & Ga. Railway.	Union Passenger Depot....	0.25
Sunset Rock	Incline and Nar. Gauge R'ys..	Horse Cars and Union R'y.	0.25

*Make contracts with hackmen. Usual charge, one dollar an hour.

LANDMARKS OF WAR TIMES.

Headquarters Gen. Rosecrans. Now 316 Walnut street.

Headquarters Gen. Bragg. "Brabson House," now 407 E. Fifth.

Headquarters Grant, Thomas, Sherman. Now 110 Walnut street.

Headquarters Gen. D. H. Hill. Now 603 Pine street.

Headquarters Gen. Brannan. S. E. cor. Third and Walnut streets.

Old War Prison (both armies). S. W. cor. Fourth and Market.

Fort Wood. East City; rapidly being covered with dwellings.

Fort Negley. Rear of Stanton House; houses going up there.

Fort Sherman, then "Brabson Hill." Fifth and Lindsay streets.

Fort Cameron. Traces of fort and magazine still on Cameron Hill.

Signal Point. Walden's Ridge, southern projection.

Signal Rock. Lookout Mountain, near to "Point."

Crutchfield House. Read House built on site.

Planters Hotel. Wisdom House built on site.

American Hotel. Bottling house, 826 Broad street.

Kaylor Hall. Through alley between 819 and 821 Market street.

EVENTS OF 1889.

This edition of 5,000 copies of the "Guide to Chattanooga" goes to press July 1, 1889, while preparations are being made to welcome—

1. THE NATIONAL EDUCATIONAL ASSOCIATION.

This Association, composed of the Educators of the United States, will assemble in Nashville, Tenn., on July 16, and remain in session during three days. They will come to Chattanooga as excursionists, the Nashville & Chattanooga Railroad running special trains at very low rates.

Twenty-eight committees have been organized to escort those teachers to historic points in the environs, and to make them feel that Chattanooga is honored by their visit. Beyond doubt, the warm weather and the crowded condition of cars and hostelries will cause some to murmur, even in the midst of our sublime scenery, but ninety per centum of those devoted men and charming women will return to their homes, all over the Union, pleased and edified by their visit to our City of the Mountains. They will know us better, and, may we not hope, will like us the better for their seeing us in the flesh. Will it be too much to prophesy that these teachers will say to their students:

"If these Southrons do not truly love us,
And err in ignorance and not in cunning,
Then we have no judgment of honest faces."

In the native language of his own green Isle of the Ocean the writer of these lines says in true heartiness, *Cead mille falthe!*

2. THE SOCIETY OF THE ARMY OF THE CUMBERLAND.

This Society visits us again this year, on "Chickamauga Days," September 19, 20. They came to us once before, in 1881, the history of which visit is given elsewhere in this "Guide."

The writer of these lines organized a Society of ex-Confederates to greet those gallant visitors in 1881, and a "Camp" of the Confederate Veterans will welcome them just as heartily next September.

Every arrangement is being made for the comfort and entertainment of the Veterans who fought on both sides at Chickamauga and at Missionary Ridge. At no point in the Union could this reunion and commingling be as thorough, hearty, and sincere as at Chattanooga. Here partisans forget their folly, and bigots deny their former narrowness with shamefacedness. In Chattanooga our chiefest boast is, WE ARE AMERICAN CITIZENS!

Gentlemen of the Society of the Army of the Cumberland, and of the various Confederate Associations, we greet thee. Silver and gold have we little, but we have hearts that are big, and a welcome that ever smiles. Chattanooga boasts as liberal, active, hospitable, and unselfish a population as any town on the American continent. Gladly do we welcome all good people from every section of the civilized globe who come to our city to make an honest living, and acquire a fortune by honorable means. If you like us, cast your lot in with us, and grow old, rich and happy with the rest of us! And, in the spirit of Shakspeare's Simonides, "To say YOU are welcome would be superfluous."

IMPORTANT INFORMATION.

Readers of this Guide will file it away for reference because of the information it contains.

LEGAL HOLIDAYS.

NEW YEAR'S DAY—January 1st is a legal holiday in all the States except Arkansas, Delaware, Massachusetts, New Hampshire and Rhode Island.

WASHINGTON'S BIRTHDAY—February 22d is a legal holiday in all the States but Arkansas, Florida, Illinois, Indiana, Iowa, Kansas, Mississippi, Oregon and Tennessee.

INDEPENDENCE DAY—July 4th is a legal holiday in all the States and Territories.

CHRISTMAS DAY—December 25 is a legal holiday in all the States and Territories.

STATUTE OF LIMITATIONS.

In Tennessee, actions must be brought within years as follows:
For assault, slander, injuries, etc., within one year.
For open accounts, within six years.
For promissory notes, within six years.
For revival of judgments, within twenty years.

TAX ON COMMERCIAL TRAVELERS.

The following is a list of places and amount of taxation on commercial travelers: Alabama, $15.50 per year; Arizona, $200 per year; Beaufort, S. C., $10 per visit; Bennettsville, S. C., $1 per visit; Batesburg, S. C., 75 cents per day; Charleston, S. C., $10 per month; Cumberland, Md., $1 per day; Delaware, $25 per year; Deadwood, D. T., $5 per week; Darlington, S. C., $1; East St. Louis, $2 per day; Elkton, Md., per cent on stock carried; Florida, $25 per year; Hartwell, Ga., $5 per trip; Johnston, S. C., 50 cents per day; Lewistown, Idaho, $5 per trip; Montana, $100 per year for each county; Memphis, Tenn., $10 per week or $25 per month; Mobile, Ala., $3 per day or $7 a week; Natchez, Miss., 25 cents per day; New Orleans, La., $50 per year; Newport, Ky., $1 per month; North Carolina, $100 per year; Nevada, $100 per year; Orangeburg, S. C., $2 per day; St. Matthews, S. C., $1 per day; San Francisco, Cal., $25 per quarter; Texas, $35 a year; Tucson, Arizona, $50 per quarter; Tombstone, Arizona, $10 per day; Virginia, $75 per year; Wilmington, N. C., $3 per day; Washington, D. C., $200 per year; Walhalla, S. C., $1 per day.

SOME POSTAL FACTS.

Post-offices in Tennessee June 30, 1889.................................. 2,102
Post-offices in Tennessee of first class.................................... 4
    (1) Nashville, salary of postmaster...............................$3,400
    (2) Memphis,   "   "   3,400
    (3) Chattanooga, "   "   3,100
    (4) Knoxville,   "   "   3,000

RATES OF POSTAGE.

Letters.—Prepaid by stamps, 2 cents each ounce or fraction thereof to all parts of the United States and Canada; forwarded to another post-office without charge on request of the person addressed; if not called for, returned to the writer free, if indorsed with that request. For registering letters the charge is 10 cents additional. Drop letters at letter-carrier offices, 2 cents per ounce or fraction thereof; at other offices, 1 cent per ounce or fraction thereof.

Second Class Matter.—Periodicals issued at regular intervals—at least four times a year—and having a regular list of subscribers, with supplement, sample copies, 1 cent a pound; periodicals, other than weekly, if delivered by letter-carrier, 1 cent each; if over 2 ounces, 2 cents each. When sent by other than publishers, for 4 ounces or less, 1 cent.

Third Class Matter (not exceeding 4 pounds).—Printed matter, books, proof-sheets (corrected or uncorrected), unsealed circulars, inclosed so as to admit of easy inspection without cutting cords or wrapper, 1 cent for each 2 ounces.

Fourth Class Matter.—Not exceeding 4 pounds, embracing merchandise and samples, excluding liquids, poisons, greasy, inflammable or explosive articles, live animals, insects, etc., 1 cent an ounce. Postage to Canada and British North American States, 2 cents per ounce; must be prepaid; otherwise, 6 cents.

MATTERS OF BUSINESS.

PROMISSORY NOTES.—A note dated on Sunday is void. A note obtained by fraud, or from one intoxicated, is void. If a note be lost or stolen, it does not release the maker, he must pay it. An endorser of a note is exempt from liability, if not served with notice of its dishonor within twenty-four hours of its non payment. A note by a minor is void. Notes bear interest only when so stated. Principals are responsible for their agents. Each individual in partnership is responsible for the whole amount of the debts of the firm.

LETTERS OF RECOMMENDATION should be given cautiously. They should be both clear and candid. If a party is not worthy of a commendation, do not seem to commend by ambiguous phrases. A party may be commended for one quality, and not for others. Say what you mean or say nothing.

FOREIGN CITIES.

The following tables will be valuable to thousands who keep this Guide to Chattanooga convenient for reference. Postage given is for letters weighing half an ounce or less. Mileage is *via* New York.

DISTANCES FROM CHATTANOOGA

To	Miles.	Days in Transit.	Postage.	To	Miles.	Days in Transit.	Postage.
Alexandria	6,850	16	5	Gibraltar	5,850	15	5
Antwerp	4,700	13	5	Glasgow	4,070	12	5
Aspinwall	3,005	10	5	Hague	4,645	12	5
Athens	6,380	16	5	Havana	2,100	5	5
Barbadoes	2,840	10	5	Havre	4,630	10	5
Berlin	5,085	12	5	London	4,405	10	5
Bombay	10,465	29	5	Mexico City	2,036	5	5
Bordeaux	5,082	12	5	Paris	4,700	10	5
Bremen	5,035	12	5	Rome	5,704	13	5
Brussels	4,670	12	5	*Shanghai	10,700	36	5
Buenos Ayres	8,725	4	5	Suez	7,000	17	5
Cape Town	11,940	30	15	Vera Cruz	3,200	13	5
Calcutta	11,815	30	5	Venice	5,450	14	5
Constantinople	6,510	16	5	Vienna	5,420	12	5
Dublin	4,010	9	5	*Valparaiso	6,600	20	5
Frankfort	4,950	12	5	*Yokohama	9,400	28	5
Geneva	5,105	12	5	Zurich	5,150	13	5

*Via San Francisco.

DISTANCES FROM CHATTANOOGA

To	Miles.	Fare.	To	Miles.	Fare.
Atlanta, Ga.	138	$ 3 00	Philadelphia, Pa.	763	$20 50
Baltimore, Md.	665	17 70	Pittsburgh, Pa.	648	19 15
Boston, Mass.	1070	27 50	Richmond, Va.	592	15 25
Cincinnati, Ohio	335	9 75	San Francisco, Cal.	2736	72 50
Chicago, Ill.	599	17 00	St. Louis, Mo.	468	14 00
Indianapolis, Ind	445	12 85	St. Paul, Minn.	970	27 75
Louisville, Ky	336	9 10	Washington, D. C.	625	16 50
Memphis, Tenn.	310	9 30	Hamilton, Canada	835	23 20
Nashville, Tenn.	151	4 55	Montreal, Canada	1211	30 60
New Orleans, La.	491	14 75	Toronto, Canada	875	24 25
New York, N. Y	853	23 00	Quebec, Canada	1383	32 60
Omaha, Neb.	882	25 50	Ottawa, Canada	1058	29 50

LETTERS OF FRIENDSHIP should receive more care and thought than is generally accorded them. They should be answered promptly, and good taste should dictate the measure of freedom or formality to be observed in them.

HEALTH.

SUMMER COMPLAINTS.—In addition to ordinary prudence in diet and drink, especial care should be taken as to the quality of drinking water used. If not known to be absolutely pure, add a teaspoonful of aromatic sulphuric acid (elixir of vitriol) to one quart of water. Epidemics of cholera have been arrested, when every other means failed, by using water thus acidulated. It may be flavored with lemons and sweetened. There is good reason for believing that the cholera poison is absolutely destroyed by mineral acids. It would be well, therefore, to confine the drink exclusively to this mineral-acid lemonade so long as there is any danger of cholera. No other single precaution is of so much importance as this.

CONTAGIOUS DISEASES.—It will often relieve a mother's anxiety to know how long after a child has been exposed to a contagious disease that there is danger the disease has been contracted. The following table gives the *period of incubation*—or anxious period—and other information concerning the more important diseases:

Disease.	Symptoms usually appear	Anxious period ranges from	Patient is infectious
Chicken-pox	On 14th day	10-18 days.	Until all scabs have fallen off.
Diphtheria	" 2d "	2- 5 "	14 days after disappearance of membrane
Measles..............	" 14th "	10-14 "	*Until scaling and cough have ceased.
Mumps	" 19th "	16-24 "	14 days from commencement.
Rotheln	" 14th "	12-20 "	10 to 14 days from commencement.
Scarlet Fever........	" 4th "	1- 7 "	Until all scaling has ceased.
Small-pox	" 12th "	1-14 "	Until all scabs have fallen off.
Typhoid Fever......	" 21st "	1-28 "	Until diarrhœa ceases.
Whooping-cough....	" 14th "	7-14 "	†Six weeks from beginning to whoop.

*In measles the patient is infectious three days before the eruption appears.
†In whooping-cough the patient is infectious during the primary cough, which may be three weeks before the whooping begins.

BURNS AND SCALDS.—Dust the parts with bicarbonate of soda, or wet with water in which as much of the soda has been placed as can be dissolved. When the burns are so severe that the skin is broken and blisters raised, open the blisters at one side and swathe the parts with soft linen anointed with simple cerate or saturated with sweet oil, castor oil or equal parts of linseed oil and lime water. Burns from acids should be well washed with water. Burns from caustic alkalies should be well washed with vinegar and water. When a person's clothing is on fire he should quickly lie down and be wrapped in carpet or something else that will smother the flame.

SUNSTROKE.—Treat this by removing the clothing, applying ice to the head and arm-pits until the high temperature is lowered and consciousness returns, when it should be discontinued until a rising temperature again calls for it. A cold bath of iced water may be very beneficial.

HEMORRHAGE FROM THE NOSE may be stopped generally by snuffing up the nose salt and water, alum and water, or vinegar, or by applying ice between the shoulders, or at the back of the neck. Keep head raised.

CHATTANOOGA AS A HOME.

I cannot better close this little pamphlet than with a candid statement of a few of the surroundings of Chattanooga as a place of residence:

1. We have a balmy climate, not too hot in summer nor too cold in winter. Thermometer rarely rises above 90° or descends to 0°. Every month is pleasant except August.

2. We have mountain tops and valleys quickly reached by steam and electric transportation. These make removal to summer resorts unnecessary, and provide dry, healthful homes for consumptives.

3. We have good water, good sewerage, good schools, good fire department, good system of police, and a very energetic, pushing, reasonably moral population.

4. Chattanooga is the terminus of seven trunk lines of railway; has a belt system that connects all the railways with the factories, and reaches all the valley suburbs; has lines of railway to the summits of Lookout Mountain and Missionary Ridge, and has twenty-five miles of horse car railway.

5. Has over one hundred manufactories in successful operation, being convenient to iron, coal and timber.

6. Chattanooga has increased in population from 6,000 in 1870 to 50,000 in 1889. The increase has been remarkable during the past three years. In 1886 we had 29,000; in 1889 we have 50,000.

7. The Tennessee will be navigable from its mouth to Chattanooga by December 25, 1889, thus connecting the city by water with the Mississippi, the Ohio and the Cumberland. Then Chattanooga will have water connection with New Orleans, St. Louis, St. Paul, Cincinnati, Pittsburg and hundreds of smaller places.

8. We have good streets, the main ones laid with asphalt, Belgian blocks and creosoted bricks. They are wide and straight.

9. We have successful electric light plants, both arc and incandescent, and our main streets are lighted by electricity.

10. We have large and handsome church edifices, and enough of them to satisfy the religious peculiarities of all our citizens.

11. We have all of the popular secret societies, in full operation. All are reported in a prosperous condition.

12. Our population is made up of Northerners and Southerners, the former chiefly manufacturers, the latter wholesale and retail merchants. They are about equal in number, energy, enterprise and integrity.

These are the inducements, gentle reader, to cast in your lot with us. We do not deal in adjectives or expletives, merely recite the unadorned facts. To be sure, all people are not equally well pleased with us, but it is a fact that ninety per centum of those who in the past removed from Chattanooga in the hope of bettering their condition have returned to us.

Come and see for yourself. Make due allowance for home attachments and natural prejudices. . Everything you see will not comport with your ideas, no doubt, but, in the aggregate, you will find Chattanooga to be one of the best places to live in you have visited in any part of the Union.